John 15:14 One of Jesus' Friends

Glenn Marks

Unless the Lord Builds the House

Our Life, Love, and Labor

Sooner Copy

GLENN MARKS

Black Lake Press

TELL YOUR STORY

BLACKLAKEPRESS.COM

Cover design by Jessica Newton
Illustrations and interior design by Jessica Newton
General editorial by Cory Lakatos
Published by Black Lake Press of
Holland, Michigan

Black Lake Press is a division of
Black Lake Studio, LLC.

Direct inquiries to Black Lake Press at
www.blacklakepress.com

ISBN-13: 978-1503210479

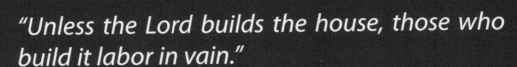

"Unless the Lord builds the house, those who build it labor in vain."

Psalm 127:1

PREFACE

Hebrews 13:7 says, "Remember your leaders, who spoke the word of God to you. Consider the outcome of their way of life and imitate their faith." I grew up in a Christian home surrounded by wonderful Christian leaders. Perhaps the most influential among them was Pastor Glenn Marks, who took an interest in my development at an early age. In fact, he knew me before I knew him. He was pioneering a new church in Lowell, Michigan, and he visited the neighborhood that my parents had recently moved into. My parents decided early in their marriage that they wanted to raise their family in a Christian home. My mom was full term in her pregnancy with me. Upon my birth, Pastor and Mrs. Marks visited us in the hospital. My parents enjoyed the warmth of their outreach and new friendship. A church was born and my mentoring began.

I enjoyed the ministry of Pastor and Mrs. Marks. Bible stories and life lessons were woven into the tapestry of my childhood. I remember being invited to participate in church services, Christmas programs, and Vacation Bible School, among other opportunities. Activities outside of church were common, too. Pastor Marks enjoyed raising ponies, and he became keenly aware of my interest in them, frequently inviting my brother and I over to teach us to ride, groom, and care for them. He seemed to always find a way to introduce life and leadership lessons into our fun times. I recall one such lesson, in which he told us of two types of trainers preparing horses for a team pulling competition. The first was a demanding taskmaster who used the whip and aggression. The other, a kind, loving master who was gentle, encouraged his team to perform and rewarded them. I learned that the physical approach produced short-term gains, but long-term results and true success were developed through earning the love, respect, and devotion of the team. Pastor Marks also taught me that leadership and parenting are both rooted in self-discipline. I remember him telling me about Napoleon, who said, "If I can control myself, I can control an army."

These lessons stuck with me when athletic teams in high school elected me as their captain, and I took them with me as I pursued my college degree. I relied on his advice when I entered military service in the United States Army, and it continued to give me guidance when I entered Officer Candidate School at Fort Benning, Georgia. I knew what kind of leader I wanted to be when I earned a commission as an officer and went on to lead infantry soldiers. I know what kind of leader I want to be as a Technical Director at a Fortune 50 company, responsible for seven states. Most importantly, I know what kind of leader I want to be as a husband and father.

Pastor Marks frequently quoted Scripture, and I remember him pointing me early in my life to Proverbs 3:5-6, which says: "Trust in The Lord with all your heart and lean not on your own understanding; in all your ways acknowledge Him and He will direct your paths." I have claimed this promise many times throughout my life, whether it was at school, work, or in relationships. I have no doubt that God blessed me as I trusted Him. I am exceedingly grateful for the Lord bringing my wife of more than twenty years into my life. We asked Pastor Marks to marry us, and one of his requirements was premarital counseling. During our sessions we covered many topics that prepared us for successful marriage and a lifetime commitment to each other. We have called upon those lessons many times as we've navigated the challenges that life has thrown at us. Pastor Marks explained that there would be struggles later on in our marriage after the "honeymoon" period was over and that we would sometimes need to make the decision to love when it might be easier to withdraw. He stressed that love is a verb, not a feeling, and that guidance has been invaluable over the years. He also told us of two brothers who chose two very different paths as they entered adulthood. One chose a life outside of the church that led to generations of failed relationships, incarceration, abuse, and other undesirable outcomes. The other chose a life of discipleship and serving Christ, which resulted in generations of Christians who went on to become successful members of society, including doctors, lawyers, teachers, etc. Pastor Marks challenged us by asking us which legacy we desired for our family. He also provided sound financial guidance for our marriage by cautioning that our success should be gauged by "the fewness of our wants, rather than the abundance of our possessions." I have oftentimes found myself sharing these words with my own children and others whom I have had the privilege of mentoring.

Pastor Marks frequently invited missionaries to visit our church and share their experiences, pictures, and stories. A seed was planted as I learned about the Great Commission from Jesus: "All authority in heaven and on earth has been given to me. Therefore go and make disciples of all nations, baptizing them in the name of the Father and of the Son and of the Holy Spirit, and teaching them to obey everything I have commanded you. And surely I am with you always, to the very end of the age" (Matthew 28:18-20). In 2004, I had the privilege of traveling overseas to my wife's native country, the Dominican Republic, on my first short-term mission trip. We built a church, conducted Bible classes for children, and held medical clinics. Since then, we have returned on multiple trips to conduct additional medical clinics and make improvements at an orphanage. It's been an amazing blessing to be a part of this and to share these experiences with my wife and three children.

While I was still young, Pastor Marks taught me the promise of James 4:7: "Submit yourselves, then, to God. Resist the devil, and he will flee from you." He coupled this verse with the additional promise of 1 Corinthians 10:13, which says, "No temptation has overtaken you except what is common to mankind. And God is faithful; he will not let you be tempted beyond what you can bear. But when you are tempted, he will also provide a way out so that you can endure it." I always knew that I had an escape, that I didn't need to succumb to life's temptations.

The guidance, mentoring, and wisdom that Pastor Marks provided to me helped me establish a solid foundation upon which to grow and develop. The biblical promises he taught me have aided me in my life's journey. I cannot forget the words of Pastor Marks, my childhood and young-adult leader, who spoke the words of God to me. I have considered his way of life and wish to imitate his faith, for I have seen his legacy. His leadership and example have influenced countless lives and will provide a positive impact on generations to come. In the words of the chorus from Steve Green's song "Find Us Faithful,"

Oh may all who come behind us find us faithful,
May the fire of our devotion light their way,
May the footprints that we leave
Lead them to believe,
And the lives we live inspire them to obey,
Oh may all who come behind us find us faithful

Timothy M. Weststrate, Sr.
Kalamazoo, Michigan
November 2014

A WORD FROM THE AUTHOR

> *"Unless the Lord builds the house, those who build it labor in vain."*
>
> Psalm 127:1

I am Glenn Marks, eighty-nine years old, and my dear wife of sixty-four years is Norma Jean. After reflecting on Psalm 90:10, we started thinking of ourselves as being old. Then Psalm 92:14 made us realize that even though death is the only end to old age, since we are still alive, we can continue to believe God for fruit. We hope this book will be part of that fruit as people read it and are challenged to more fully yield to Jesus and to more completely trust Him. The purpose of this book is to bring glory to Jesus, and we hope it will be interesting, informative, and challenging. Our desire is to make Jesus as big as possible and Glenn and Norma Jean as small as possible.

Norma Jean Byers, a true city girl from California, and Glenn Marks, a country hick from Michigan, were miraculously brought together in 1946 at Fort Wayne Bible Institute. After transferring to Bethel College and graduating in 1950, we were married and entered the ministry. Now we have had more than sixty-four wonderful years together serving Jesus. We were able to plant five churches and help dozens of congregations with building projects. Also, Norma Jean and I have been able to raise four children, help them by prayer and faith to find wonderful spouses, and to encourage our fourteen grandchildren to find Jesus as their personal Savior and to study and work hard. It truly has been an exciting journey. We want to share with you some of the things that have shaped our lives, and the ways our Heavenly Father has guided and blessed us.

As I write this book, I have been praying the prayer that I have prayed so often during my life. It is found in Psalm 139:23-24: "Search me, O God, and know my heart: try me, and know my thoughts: And see if there be any wicked way in me, and lead me in the way everlasting."

I believe I am being totally honest when I say that I consider this book to be the biggest and most important project of my entire life. I want my readers to know this: If all of us can believe that we are just a voice, a personality, and ultimately a tool for the Holy Spirit to use, we will be amazed and exceedingly thankful for what we have been privileged to be a part of for the Kingdom of God. In our life and ministry, it has been the Lord who has built the house, and that is how we know we haven't labored in vain.

TIMELINE

1925: I was born near Union, MI.

1925: Norma Jean's parents and grandparents moved to California.

1926: My family moved to Angle Streams near Union, MI.

1927: Norma Jean was born in San Diego, CA.

1933: Norma Jean attended grades 1-3 in Youngstown, OH.

1938: Norma Jean attended grade 4 in Pittsburg, PA.

1939: Norma Jean attended grade 5 in Wyandot, MI.

1940: Norma Jean attended grades 7-8 in Chicago, IL.

1942: Norma Jean attended grade 9 in Wheaton, IL.

1943: Norma Jean attended grades 10-12 in Nyack, NY.

1944: I entered the U.S. Army.

1945: Norma Jean's family moved to Claridon, OH.

1946: I returned from Europe and went to Fort Wayne Bible Institute. Norma Jean arrived the same year.

1947: I transfered to Bethel College.

1948: Norma Jean transfered to Bethel College.

1950: We graduated from Bethel and got married. We started our first church plant in Plymouth, IN.

1952: Our first daughter, Dorothy, was stillborn. We started our second church plant in South Bend, IN.

1953: Our daughter Jeannette was born.

1954: We started our third church plant in North Manchester, IN.

1956: Our daughter Marlene was born.

1959: Our son Tom was born. We started our fourth church plant in Indianapolis, IN.

1960: Our daughter Cindy was born.

1966: We pastored an established church in Pontiac, MI.

1967: We moved to Meadowview Farm.

1971: We built our home at Oak Hill. I started as associate pastor at Good Shepherd Missionary Church.

1976: We started our fifth church plant in Lowell, MI.

2003: I retired as a pastor.

2013: We moved to Hubbard Hill Asisted Living in Elkhart, IN.

GLENN MARKS FAMILY TREE

John George Dietrich
Birth: 4-24-1838
Death: 10-23- 1916

Jennie Diethrich
Birth: 12-26-1868
Death: 9-19-1949

Harriet Ritter
Birth: 9-02-1847
Death: 10-25-1924

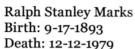

Ralph Stanley Marks
Birth: 9-17-1893
Death: 12-12-1979

Henry Marks
Birth: 10-30-1830
Death: 3-01-1898

John Henry Marks
Birth: 12-08-1864
Death: 2-14-1946

Angeline Arnold
Birth: 10-30-1826
Death: 7-12-1907

Glenn Herbert Marks
Birth: 7-27-1925

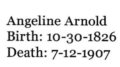

David Holdeman
Birth: 6-29-1864
Death: 7-02-1941

Samuel Holdeman
Birth: 11-30-1819
Death: 8-07-1899

Sarah Boyer
Birth: 1-27-1827
Death: 8-29-1880

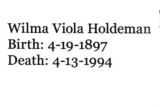

Wilma Viola Holdeman
Birth: 4-19-1897
Death: 4-13-1994

Daniel Stump
Birth: 7-15-1840
Death: 8-29-1880

Hannah Stump
Birth: 10-12-1868
Death: 12-14-1942

Sarah Snoke
Death: 1871

NORMA JEAN BYERS FAMILY TREE

Thomas VanScoic Byers
Birth: 4-05-1866
Death: 1-10-1958

Benjamin Franklin Byers
Birth: 2-16-1837
Death: 2-13-1923

Mary Elizabeth Bowmen
Birth: 2-16-1837
Death: 2-04-1923

Donald Wendel Byers
Birth: 6-28-1902
Death: 2-28-1994

Laura Gertrude Thompson
Birth: 1-29-1874
Death: 12-21-1960

Robert Mahlon Thompson
Birth: 10-20-1846
Death: 5-30-1933

Mary Catherine White
Birth: 9-10-1850
Death: 5-25-1940

Norma Jean Byers
Birth: 11-21-1927

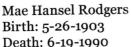

Andrew Rodgers
Birth: 8-16-1866
Death: 11-01-1916

John Rodgers
Birth: 1841
Death: 1881

Eliza Jane Adair
Birth: 1846
Death: 1918

Mae Hansel Rodgers
Birth: 5-26-1903
Death: 6-19-1990

Martha Virginia Rhoads
Birth: 1868
Death: 1929

John R Rhoads
Birth: 1839

Elizabeth
Birth: 1842

INTRODUCTION

"With my mouth, I will make your faithfulness known through all generations. I will declare that your love stands firm forever, that you established your faithfulness in heaven itself."

Psalm 89:1b-2

"Stanley, Stanley! It's time to call the doctor!"

The country doctor had given my mother strict instructions not to deliver her fourth child without him present. However, July 27, 1925, in Union, Michigan, was a perfect day for fishing. When the time came for my birth, the doctor had gone fishing and could not be found. So, with only the help of my mother's younger sister, I was born.

My three-and-a-half-year-old brother, Donald, did not really want a baby brother. He tried to escape all of the fuss by climbing the thirty-foot ladder to the top of the windmill and giving everyone a good scare. My sisters, Joy and Esther, on the other hand, were delighted and welcomed my arrival.

This is how my life began, and this book is the rest of the story, as best as I can remember and recount it. Just as when I was born, my life did not always go as expected or planned. Though I was welcomed by many, there were times of disappointment and rejection. However, I received the love and salvation of Jesus Christ at an early age and have known His goodness, mercy, and faithfulness each step of the way.

My mother and I when I was three months old.

MAKING IT THROUGH THE GREAT DEPRESSION

In the mid-1920s, my parents, Stanley and Wilma, were farming with Daddy's grandfather. This was going quite well. The carpentry business, however, was really booming. At that time, my father made the decision to go into the carpentry business with his father, John. Grandpa John and Grandma Jenny lived at a place affectionately called "Angle Stream" in Cass County. It was named Angle Stream because of the winding creek that flowed behind the barn. The property had a large, white farmhouse, a workshop, corn crib, granary, and a chicken house. My father and grandfather built a small addition to the carpenter shop that would make a temporary home for my family and would eventually become valuable space for the expanding carpentry business. Daddy and Grandpa John made plans for a new house in the west lot, and they collected a considerable amount of lumber for the new home. In 1929, however, the stock market crashed, leading to the Great Depression. This changed everything. The booming carpentry business dried up, and the new home was never completed.

Instead, we continued to live in the 16'x24' addition. My two older sisters slept in the upstairs of my grandparents' house, but our family of six lived in that small addition. Despite the tight space, we had comfortable furniture that came from Grandpa and Grandma Diethrich. The tiny home was clean and neat because my mother was an excellent housekeeper. When my baby sister Alta was born, my brother and I started sleeping in the other upstairs bedroom in the house. As time passed and my two older sisters were in high school, they got jobs in people's homes and would live at home only on the weekends.

Despite the Depression, the Lord took care of us beautifully. My parents were always thankful we had a warm, dry place to live. Although there were hard times happening around us, we had a good life. I never felt as if we were poor. I do remember eating several dinners that consisted of only bread and milk, but I was never hungry. I always had clean clothes to wear, even if they were patched.

Recreation was not totally out of our lives. My Daddy really enjoyed playing croquet with a croquet set given to him. It was during the Depression that he got the idea of constructing a permanent croquet court. He harnessed up the horses, and they pulled the plow and grate to make a very level piece of ground. Daddy found beautiful stones from the family lake property and used them to line one end of the court. All the stakes and arches were put up. Whenever we could spare the time, we grabbed the mallets and balls stored in the smoke house and enjoyed playing a game. I have always felt that the hours of playing croquet developed our hand-eye coordination and helped us later in life to work quickly and efficiently.

Most of the time, though, my Daddy worked tremendously hard, doing anything imaginable to earn a living. He even started a butchering business. People from all around the Union area would bring their pigs to be butchered on our farm. In the springtime, Daddy tapped over fifty maple trees in Grandpa John's woods to make maple syrup to sell. When my grandfather, George Diethrich, died, Daddy was able to bring a team of horses, a wagon, and the best of the farm equipment back to his place. So, even though we had very few acres, we had what it took to maintain our cows, pigs, horses, and chickens. We grew hay, corn, and vegetables. We also had potatoes and beans in a big garden by the creek. The cows stayed healthy and gave us plenty of milk and meat. We also separated the milk using a special machine and sold cream. With the Lord's provision and hard work, our family survived the Depression.

Top: My siblings Don, Joy, Esther, and I in 1928.
Middle: Chapel Hill school.
Bottom Left: Myself, eight years old, with a calf.
Bottom Right: My siblings and I in 1934.

GROWING UP ON ANGLE STREAM FARM

From my earliest recollection, life was very happy in our "little home" at Angle Stream. We had all we needed and plenty to keep us busy. Family was always around to help with work or play, or just to talk. Since we lived in the same yard as my Grandma and Grandpa Marks, I spent a lot of time with them.

I started very young helping Grandma feed and take care of the chickens. I would turn the crank on the corn sheller for Grandma, then we would mix the corn, wheat, and oats and throw it out for the chickens to eat. We had to make sure a box in the henhouse had oyster shells in it so the chickens could eat those to help them digest the grain. We would usually gather about a dozen eggs each day.

Raising baby chicks was another part of our job. When an old hen would want to "set" on the nest-egg box, we would scribble pencil marks on a dozen eggs and put them under her. If she laid another egg, we could take it out. This way all the eggs would hatch at the same time. In about twenty days we would have a dozen baby chicks. Grandma had five or six little galvanized houses that we would put together. We would bring mama and her babies up to the back yard and put them in her house. The first couple of days they would live in the house and a very small enclosure in front of it. After that they would run free in the yard and fields during the day and be shut in the house at night. There were a lot of chicken hawks around. The instant she would hear the hawk whistle, the hen would give a certain cluck and all the babies would dash under her wings. We would raise sixty to eighty chicks per year.

I really enjoyed being around the barn. Grandpa had built it to accommodate two horses, three cows, and a place to store the buggy. He had one white horse named Carl and one black cow named Ebony. Carl was later replaced by a Model T, and the buggy was just pushed outside for us kids to play in. We also had two horses, a bay named Daisy and a gray named Roxy, that had belonged to Grandpa Dietrich. They were both very willing horses: Roxy was willing to pull, and Daisy was willing to let her! We always needed to urge Daisy to keep up her end.

I loved to go down in the barn and sit on the horse's back, and I was permitted to do it even when I was very small. I could climb up on the manger, hang onto the slots in the center partition, get back to the flat part, and then get on the horse's back. In the wintertime it was not unusual to find a couple of barn cats on the horse's back. Imagine my glory sitting on this big work horse, petting a cat. This was one of my favorite getaway places for quite a long time.

The three cow stalls were filled with Lil in the south, Ebony in the middle, and Patsy in the north stall. Daddy milked Lil, Grandpa milked Ebony, and Don milked Patsy. I learned to milk on Patsy, too. When I started to milk, Grandpa Marks stopped coming down. While we were milking, the cats

The Stanley Marks Family—Esther, Don, Joy in back, me, Stanley, Wilma, and Alta in front.

always stood close by, hoping we would squirt milk in their mouths, which we always did.

One of the rewards of milking was Grandma's graham cracker box. She kept it on the shelf right above the clean milk bucket. It always seemed so natural to take a couple of crackers and eat them on the way to the barn. A word was never spoken as far as I know, but Grandma must have enjoyed it as much as we did, or she could have certainly found another place to keep her crackers.

After milking, we carried the milk to the house and strained it into the tank on the top of a DeLaval separator. This was quite a complicated machine. It had about a dozen disks that went inside a cone-shaped bowl, and a nut tightened down on top. When we turned the crank on the separator the correct number of turns per minute (I've forgotten just how many), we opened the valve to the tank, and the milk ran into the spinning bowl. There were two spouts around this bowl, and cream would come out of one, and the skim milk out the other. Twice a week a truck from the Constantine Creamery would come around and pick up the cream. The driver would leave the boxes of butter we needed and pay us for the rest of the cream. We fed the skim milk to the calves and pigs. Five milking cows were the most I remember having at any one time.

One of my self-appointed fun jobs was to teach the little calves to lead. I spent many hours leading them around, brushing them, hugging them, and letting them know that they were expected to be tame, gentle members of our bovine herd.

I especially enjoyed working with my Grandpa John, and it is a real privilege to write about him. He was a finish carpenter. At a very young age he put a little hammer in my hand, gave me a block of wood and a little cup of nails, and let me pound away. Other times he would give me a small shovel and ask me to move the sawdust from under the saw to over by the wood stove so he could burn it.

Grandpa Marks was quite a small man, and he wasn't in very good health. His mind was very sharp, though, and using the little numbers on the carpenter square, he could cut the complete set of roof rafters for any type of roof. He must have liked school, as he took a special interest in writing and had excellent penmanship. When farther along in school, he would write essays. He also took part in debates and seemed to enjoy them. He became a good reader and always kept up with the news of the day. He was excellent in spelling, good in figures, and he always kept a record of his work. He had records of ninety-plus buildings that he had built in the neighborhood and a thousand saws that he had filed (sharpened). If asked his business he would say, "My business is serving the Lord, and I drive nails for a living." Grandpa never really talked to me about spiritual things, but he lived them.

Left: Some horses and I when I was a young man. Right: Tending cows at Angle Stream around 1944.

MY SPIRITUAL HERITAGE

Over and over again I thank God for the spiritual heritage passed down to me from my parents and grandparents. They laid the foundation upon which my own faith would be built. This is a brief history of that heritage, the church I grew up in, and how it started.

Around 1900, a local minister in the Mennonite Church by the name of Daniel Brenneman experienced a dramatic change in his spiritual life. He began holding evangelistic meetings in schoolhouses wherever he could. The movement caught on in the area. Other ministers also began holding Sunday Schools, Sunday evening services, and even camp meetings. The movement was founded on the belief that there is more to our relationship with God than just form or tradition. We can have a true personal relationship with our Savior, Jesus Christ! Largely because of the strong evangelical focus, the group became known as the New Mennonites, and eventually the Mennonite Brethren in Christ.

The hearts of many were touched by these special meetings, including my mother's parents, David and Hannah Holdeman. They became more devoted to Christ, and their lives were changed. God was starting something wonderful in the small community around Union, Michigan.

In 1908, Rev. Mahlon Carmichael, a minster who was part of this movement and had served briefly out west, moved back into the area. He bought an old mill that was in disrepair, worked hard to restore it, and got it back in operation. My mother and her siblings, who happened to hear Rev. Carmichael teaching Bible stories at a camp meeting, were very surprised one day to see him driving a team of horses as they were walking to school. They excitedly told their parents about seeing him. David and Hannah were curious about this minister who could also work with his hands, and a friendship soon began.

Rev. Carmichael held evangelical meetings in big tents at the restored mill. The meetings were well attended, and in May of 1910, the growing group felt they needed a larger place to hold the two weeks of revival services they were planning. Chapel Hill Community Church, affectionately called the Old Log Church, was chosen, and Emma Landert, an approved "Ministering Sister," preached the Gospel messages at those meetings. Among those hearing the Gospel message for the first time were my father, Stanley, and his father, John Marks. They made a commitment to Christ at those meetings, and their lives were changed. Many were baptized at the mill, and soon after, regular services were held in the Old

Left: David and Hannah Holdeman with their family in 1910. Right: Old Log Church.

Log Church.

On February 5, 1911, Rev. Carmichael helped to formally organize the group with nine charter members. Daniel and Hannah Holdeman, with their daughter Wilma, and John Marks, with his son Stanley, were among those first charter members.

Meetings continued to be held at the Old Log Church. It was shared with the Quakers, who used it on Sunday mornings. Each group respected the other. They each had their own woodpile and supply of kerosene. This went on for about ten years until everyone got tired of trying to keep two busy congregations in one small log building. The Grange Hall in Union wanted to build a bigger hall. John had been a member of that lodge, so our group got the old building. It was loaded onto rollers, pulled with a team of horses, and moved two and a half miles up to the new site, which was right across from the Old Log Church. A stonemason was hired, everyone brought surplus rocks from their farms, and the basement walls were built under it on site. It was named simply Chapel Hill Church.

Wilma and Stanley, my parents, were married in 1915 and faithfully attended Chapel Hill Church with their children, giving sacrificially of their time and resources to support the church and share the Gospel that had changed their lives. Our congregation was a group of simple country folk, devoted and dedicated to our Lord and Savior Jesus Christ. The whole ministry of the church was designed to lead its members into a deep and thorough knowledge and experience of the Christian life. We supported Christian education and the work of missionaries in Africa, as well.

For the centennial celebration of the Chapel Hill Church in 2011, I did some research and discovered that about two hundred of its members had actively served the Lord in vocational ministry over that hundred-year period. I am sure my own ministry of organizing meetings to start new churches had its roots in that group and the spiritual fruit it bore in the lives of my parents and grandparents.

Above: John and Jennie Marks with their son Stanley.
Left: Chapel Hill Church.

MY EDUCATION AND FUTURE PLANS

I attended a one-room schoolhouse for grades one through eight. It was one mile from our home, next to the Chapel Hill Church. I will never forget my teacher, Miss Neva Mallo. She was my only teacher for all eight years! I was the only one in my grade most years, so when I graduated from eighth grade, I could honestly say, "I graduated at the top of my class!" After that I attended high school in Bristol, Indiana. It was about seven miles away, but a dollar a week, which would buy five gallons of gas, got me a ride with some neighbor boys. I enjoyed those four years and graduated in the spring of 1943.

My parents wanted me to be a carpenter like Grandpa Marks. I knew I didn't like carpentry work, even though I did it for my first paying job as a teenager, making ten cents an hour. I didn't want to be a carpenter. Given a choice between the two, I would rather have been a farmer.

I'm embarrassed to admit it, but eventually I got into an argument with my parents about this. I was a teenager, and America was closer to getting caught up in the war in Europe. I told my parents, "I'd rather go fight Hitler than be a carpenter." With our Mennonite background, I'm sure that must have hurt them. They didn't respond, which makes me feel even more embarrassed looking back on it. It was terribly disrespectful.

Even though I would have rather been a farmer than a carpenter, the truth is that I wasn't sure that either was right for me. I understood enough to know that there's more to life than just physical things; that spiritual goals and accomplishments matter more. Quite early in my life I sincerely wanted whatever the Lord had in store for me. I began to sense that God made all of us differently, and that the more I tied my life in with the Almighty God's purposes, and the more I let him guide my life, the better off it was going to be. I had ups and downs in my spiritual life, but I wanted God's direction. I wanted to do his will, whatever that might mean and wherever that might take me. I felt this as a child, and very strongly by the time I was a teenager.

Even though I was open to whatever He wanted, I felt drawn to the ministry. Two of my aunts and one of my sisters had gone to Fort Wayne Bible Institute, and I thought that maybe the Lord could use me in the ministry.

But other forces were in motion.

Since I was born in 1925, I was fourteen when Hitler invaded Poland. In the years leading up to that, we heard bits and pieces about the war that was brewing in Europe. Grandpa Marks had a radio in his place, a very early unit that seemed old even then. Since our house was nearby, we heard various news reports. Because of our denominational background, which had some Mennonite mixed in, we had a rather pacifist attitude toward current events. But it was becoming hard to ignore the growing bad news. We knew Hitler was dangerous, and that the country could get caught up in the conflict in Europe. I think the Battle of Britain in 1940—hearing the stories of the bombs falling on London and the English pilots trying to fight them off—made more of an impression on us than perhaps even Pearl Harbor did the following year.

America entered the war after the attack on Pearl Harbor in 1941. I was still only sixteen, but other young men were leaving to serve. I remember that a local boy was killed in North Africa, and it was quite a shock to our small community. It really brought the whole thing closer to home.

Sugar and other items were being rationed for the war effort, so we were all very aware of how it was impacting our lives. Young men were going away, some enlisting and some being drafted. Despite our pacifist inclinations, we didn't object to them serving however the Lord worked it out. My brother and I had the sense that we probably would be serving soon. Despite my greater sense that the Lord might use me in the ministry, I always wanted to do my part in anything that needed to be done. If that meant military service, I wanted to be in there doing my part.

HONESTY IS THE BEST POLICY

This is a statement I heard very early in life. Learning to be honest and to make restitution was a big part of my childhood. It was a message I picked up both at home and through the preaching at church. With this combination, truth was not only taught but "caught."

Even small amounts are very important: "Whoever can be trusted with very little can also be trusted with much, and whoever is dishonest with very little will also be dishonest with much" (Luke 16:10, ESV). Jesus also said in his parable in Luke 19:17, "'Well done, my good servant!' his master replied. 'Because you have been trustworthy in a very small matter, take charge of ten cities.'"

For example, once when I was about seven I picked up a fifty cent piece off the table at my neighbor's house and put it in my pocket. I felt guilty, but I didn't do anything about it. Then the minister at church talked about not stealing, and also making it right if we had stolen. I could get no peace. I realized what I had done was wrong, but I struggled for a long time. Finally, I went back over there, gave the fifty cents back, and told them I was sorry. It was hard to do, but I was happy and relieved afterwards.

There was another time when Daddy wanted some material from a man, so Mother gave me thirty-five cents to give to him. He refused to take it, so I kept that thirty-five cents. That bothered me. I was convicted, and I had to tell my mother I was sorry and make it right.

Being honest was also a big part of my teenage years. When I was in high school, I rode with some other kids to school. One day the other kids wanted to go to a movie, and we got permission to leave school and drive into Elkhart to the movie theater. We were late getting home. I knew my parents would not approve of leaving school and going to a movie, so I told them we had car trouble. It wasn't the truth, and I had to get peace in my heart by telling my folks exactly what happened.

For a few years, while I was building churches, I had my own company. I remember so clearly doing my income taxes during the first year. I became aware of an area where I thought it questionable whether I needed to pay income tax. Eventually, I came to the conclusion that I would much rather have God's blessing than the few dollars I could have saved by doing something questionable. God prospered my business so it met the financial needs of my family and helped several churches save a lot of money on their buildings. Honesty truly is the best policy.

THE MODEL T

When things were going well before the Depression, my Grandfather Marks retired the family horse and buggy and bought a new 1925 Ford Model T. We nicknamed it "Old Lizzie." This car was some piece of equipment! If you wanted to go, all you had to do was make sure it had gas and oil, and oil a few parts with a squirt oil can. You set the emergency brake that put it in neutral, raised the spark lever, and lowered the gas lever. Then you went out front and pulled the choke lever and started the crank. (You did not grip the crank with your thumb, lest Old Lizzie kicked and broke your thumb.)

When she started, you ran to the controls as fast as you could to pull down (advance) the spark with the choke and gas lever to keep her running, and take your place as the "big shot" in the driver's seat. On a very cold or damp morning, Lizzie started better if the four coils that made the spark had been kept in the oven of the kitchen wood stove all night.

You were now ready for your journey. All you had to do was release the emergency brake, push down on the gas pedal a little, push the center pedal to put the car in "reverse," back out of the barn, and push the left pedal all the way down to put it in "low" and get moving forward. When you were moving at a sufficient speed, you let up on the pedal, and that was "high."

Our top speed was about 30-35 miles per hour. Old Lizzie had a canvas top and canvas side curtains with isinglass windows to help keep out the wind and cold. Heaters had not been perfected yet, so we needed a lot of blankets to keep warm.

Grandpa and Daddy drove the Model T to work. They made a trailer to haul ladders, tools, lumber, and other needed supplies. It also took the family to Elkhart for shopping, and to church and camp meeting. Sometime during the early 30s, Old Lizzie wore out and was replaced with a Buick roadster, the car with a reputation of being able to pass everything but a gas station.

MEMORIES OF GRANDPA DAVID AND GRANDMA HANNAH HOLDEMAN

My earliest memories are of family gatherings at Grandpa and Grandma Holdeman's eighty-acre farm, which was about a mile north of Union, Michigan. We spent a lot of holidays with them and would quite frequently go there after church on Sunday. Aunts Ella and Grace and Uncle Paul, all single, lived there, too. The meals were always very, very good. Grandma and Aunt Grace usually fixed fried chicken, homemade noodles, mashed potatoes and gravy, a canned or fresh vegetable from the garden, and red tapioca pudding with whipped cream. That was my favorite dessert, and I can still see and taste it. Of course, there was always homemade bread with real butter and jam or jelly.

After this big dinner, I remember going into the front part of the living room and lying on the rug that was made from the skin of a pet dog. I liked to lie there and look at the pictures in their three dimension viewer. They had wooden puzzles, marbles, and little things we could play with. We liked to play on the large porch that was on the front and both sides of the house.

When there was a whole gang of grandchildren, we would play Anti-I-Over. We would choose sides, and one group would get on one side of the house, with the other group on the other side. One side would have a ball and throw it over the house, saying, "Anti-I-Over." If the other side caught the ball, they would sneak around the house and try to hit a player. When someone was hit, that person had to join the other team. We would play until everyone was on one team.

Croquet was a lot of fun at Grandpa and Grandma's. They had a real nice place on the side of the house. As I remember, the men and older kids would get very serious about the game and do some pretty fancy stuff. Sometimes we would go out to the clean part of the barnyard and play "workup," a simplified

My Grandpa David and Grandma Hannah Holdeman. The little girl is my mother, Wilma.

version of softball.

When I was very young, I remember going out with Grandpa to do chores. He fed the horses, Queenie and Nell, the big and smaller pigs, and the cows. I watched him milk the cows, separate the milk, and feed the calves the skimmed milk. I really enjoyed being with Grandpa.

Grandma and Grandpa Holdeman's house.

When I got a little older, I started to help him. It seemed as if about every time I was over there, Grandpa wanted to sharpen a tool, and I got to turn the big grindstone for him. Sometimes during the year he had to clean his wheat and oat seeds. I would turn the crank on the fanning mill. This big, box-like machine had screens that would shake and a wind tunnel that the seeds would fall through. When we were finished the chaff and weed seeds were gone and the largest kernels were ready to plant.

I was probably only six years old when I started to drive the horses to load hay. I never figured it out until I was much older, but if I was not driving right, Grandpa would just holler "Gee" or "Haw" and the horses would obey him. I also led Queenie on the rope to pull the hay up into the mow. I really felt I was a big help to him, but much later I realized that if I was not there, the horse would do it by herself at Grandpa's voice commands. He was a very wise

man, and I learned a principle that I used with my children and grandchildren.

The whole family would help Grandpa shock the grain. The binder was some piece of equipment! It would cut the grain, carry it on a moving canvas to one side, tie it into bundles, and drop it on a carrier. The carrier was dumped in straight rows when it got four to six bundles on it. The bundles had to be set up in shocks to dry for about six weeks before they could be threshed. You started with four bundles in the center, put two bundles on each side, spread out both ends of one bundle, and put it on for a cap like a thatched roof. If you did it right, the shock would not be blown over by the wind, the cap would keep the rain out, and the grain would dry and be ready to thresh.

Threshing day was always a highlight of the year. As a child, I was the water boy; I would pump cold water into the gallon thermos jug and head out to give everyone in the twenty-plus man crew a drink from the same jug. It doesn't sound too appetizing or sanitary in our times, but no one worried about it then. The three Smith brothers had a big steam engine and a large separator that they would bring to the farm. It took about seven wagons hauling grain to keep the rig running at capacity. the farmers would go together in "rings" so they would have enough help on threshing day. It would usually take half a day at each place. The steam engine and separator would stay in a community until every farm in the "ring" was done. The ladies would go together and fix the dinner. This was always a really big feast. Grandma's was always one of the places where they ate, so I got to be part of that wonderful event.

When I was ten or so, I began plowing (cultivating) corn for Grandpa. The corn was planted in straight rows far enough apart so the horses could walk between and pull the cultivator. Grandpa could drive the horses in a straight line, but there was also a wire with knots on it that tripped the planter so the rows would be straight in both directions. The corn had to be plowed in one direction, and then a few days later in the other direction. The cultivator had two gangs of shovels with a handle on each gang. I would walk behind and guide these gangs close to the plants to take out the weeds but not harm the plants themselves.

I was starting to enjoy the cultivating quite a bit, but one day, while working in the back field, I saw a squirrel run up a tree and into a nest. I got curious and tried to climb the tree to see the nest. I stepped on a dead limb that snapped off. I fell and broke my arm. It had to be set, and I couldn't use it for about three weeks. I felt so bad that I couldn't help Grandpa for the rest of the summer.

Grandpa's farm was a beauty to behold! He worked hard to keep the buildings in good shape and the huge yard mowed and weed-free. The fields were level and the soil was good. Corn, wheat, oats, and alfalfa were grown. Grandpa rotated the crops so that each field would be in grass once every seven years and could enjoy its biblical Sabbath.

At the edge of the lane that went back into the fields was a huge stone pile. I remember helping Grandpa pick up stones from the fields, throwing them into the wagon, and dumping them by the side of the field. Years later, before the farm was sold, I went back to that stone pile and chose about a dozen stones of different sizes and shapes. When I built our home at Oak Hill, I split those stones and used them in the stone front of the house. The memories of my grandparents and their farm, like those stones, have a humble beauty and have brought much joy to me over the years.

Our home at Oak Hill with stones from Grandpa Holdeman's farm.

FAMILY SAYINGS

1. Don't cry over spilled milk.

2. The man who never made a mistake, never did anything.

3. Where there's a will, there's a way.

4. Necessity is the mother of invention, but she is not always proud of her offspring.

5. If at first you don't succeed, try, try again.

6. Two heads are better than one.

7. Well begun is half done.

8. If you can dream it, you can do it.

9. "If I can control myself, I can control an army." –Napoleon

10. Even the turtle won't get anywhere unless he is willing to stick his neck out.

11. Never say never.

12. You can't tell by the size of the frog how far he will jump.

13. A stitch in time saves nine.

14. What you are speaks so loud, I can't hear what you say.

15. Don't count your chickens before they are hatched.

16. Never try to cross the bridge until you come to it.

17. God works in mysterious ways His wonders to perform.

18. The Lord guides a moving vessel.

19. If it's worth doing, it's worth doing right.

20. Consistency, thou art a jewel.

21. The prosperity of the Lord consists not in the abundance of the things we possess, but in the fewness of our wants.

22. "There is no limit to what can be accomplished by a group of men [people] if they don't care who gets the glory." —Andrew Carnegie

23. If you want a good wife, find a good mother and marry one of her daughters.

24. Faint heart never won fair lady.

YOU CAN'T TELL BY THE SIZE OF THE FROG HOW FAR HE WILL JUMP

When I was a senior in high school, we were given the opportunity to take a V-12 test, which was for the US Navy. Those who passed the test were considered applicants for a five-year enlistment and an opportunity to become naval officers. One other classmate and I passed the test, and I was scheduled for a physical. I got on the bus to go to the big city of Indianapolis, Indiana. That was quite an adventure, since I had done very little traveling in my life thus far.

I got to the recruiting station just before noon. Some officer had figured out how to get a little extra money, so they looked at my ears and told me I would need to see a local doctor over the noon hour to have the wax removed from my ears. I complied with his order, had the wax removed, and returned for the lineup for my physical. As soon as the inspecting officer came in he pointed at me and said, "That man is too short." They measured me and told me to head home. At 5' 4", I was just too short.

I've always been a short man, but it really didn't bother me too much until I got into the ministry. Then Satan began to tell me that I was so short that I would never make it as a preacher. He beat me around for a while, until I remembered the words of my father. When he was a kid there was no money for games or entertainment, so they often made up games. Behind the barn there was an abundance of frogs. Each boy would capture a frog, and they would put them inside of a circle. Then the boy who could get his frog to jump out of the circle first, without touching his frog, was the winner. My father always said, "You can't tell by the size of the frog how far he will jump."

Somehow, I was able to use that statement, together with God's promises, as my help regarding being very short. It's amazing how that helped me through. I accepted my height, and that things don't always go as we want them to in life. I had begun to realize that all things worked together for good and to grab ahold of the promise that God, through Christ and the Holy Spirit, is working out our lives. I began to have confidence in the fact that the Lord knew what I needed. This is just another example of how the Holy Spirit has helped me grasp a statement or Scripture verse in order to defeat Satan.

As I have examined my life and the things that Jesus has helped me to accomplish, I am convinced that being short was an asset rather than a hindrance. I was a bashful kid if there ever was a bashful kid, and during my first call as a minister I didn't know what to say to people. That was painful for me (and, I'm sure, for them), but people weren't afraid of me. I could not assume a right to leadership or that people would listen to me because of my physical size. However, I could be myself and gain people's confidence, and that enabled me to talk with many people dealing with their own struggles. I'm convinced that I was able to serve the Lord considerably better being short than if I had been a big man. I gained confidence, and the Lord used me. Of course, the devil still beat me up from time to time. "All the leaders are the big guys. You'll never amount to anything" But my father's statement continued to help me a tremendous amount. You truly can't tell by the size of the frog how far he will jump!

WORLD WAR II

On December 7, 1941, the Japanese attacked Pearl Harbor and brought the United States into World War II. All of a sudden, young men graduating from my high school were enlisting or being drafted. I was only sixteen at the time, but my brother and I knew that we would eventually serve. I wasn't eager to fight, but I wanted to pitch in and do my part.

Our denomination had pacifist inclinations but didn't strictly oppose military service. Members had three options: We could file as "conscientious objectors," asking the government to excuse us from service altogether. We could enter the military and serve in a noncombatant role (medical, supply, administration, etc.). Or we could join one of the civilian public services, like the merchant marine.

During my senior year in high school, I heard about something that I thought might be another option for me. It was the Navy's V-12 program. If you were accepted, the Navy sent you to college to get a bachelor's degree, after which you would enter active service as an officer. It was a great opportunity to get an education, paid for by the government, and still be able to serve honorably with new skills. To enter the program, I had to take a test during my senior year. I thought it sounded interesting and exciting, so I signed up for the exam.

I was disappointed to be turned down for the program because of my height, but instead, I signed up to go to Fort Wayne Bible Institute. To make sense out of what happened next, you have to understand how the draft worked in those days. Young men had to register for the draft, giving the government all their information so they could be selected and notified when their time came. At the time that you registered for the draft, you had to declare on the form if you wanted to apply for a deferment to be excused from military service. There were different types of deferment; for example, "4-F" meant you

weren't capable because of some physical limitation or handicap. "1-O" was for conscientious objectors. Active religious ministers or pastors could apply for a "4-D." Students studying for the ministry could apply for a "2-D."

I graduated from high school in June and registered for the draft in July. But because I hadn't yet signed up for or been accepted to Fort Wayne, I didn't put "2-D" down on the draft form. Without a deferment classification, I was still eligible for the draft. I went off to Bible college and started the fall semester, but then I got a draft letter, and on January 11, 1944, I went into the United States Army.

Because of my denomination's stance on service, I requested a noncombatant role. I was sent to Camp Grant in Illinois for basic training. Camp Grant was where they trained soldiers going into the medical service. I was willing to serve in combat as a medic, and I felt that I could do my part for the war effort that way. When I got to the camp, since I had spent some time at college, they asked me if I could type. I said I could, so they put me in a clerk's typist training. I didn't especially like it, and I wasn't especially good at it. I could type, but English and spelling were never my strong points at all. I was trained as a medic and assigned to the medical department, but given a military speciality number as a "clerk typist." It certainly wasn't what I had imagined I'd be doing for the war effort, but on the other hand, clerk typists didn't get killed and didn't need to be replaced as often as some soldiers.

I did have one regret in basic training, however. The first night in the Army, at Camp Grant, I had this tremendous urge that before I crawled into my bunk I should get down on my knees and pray. But there I was, the first night of basic training, in a barrack full of men I had never met. I chickened out and didn't do it. While God in his mercy took

A few photos of me at basic training for the army.

care of me and I got along alright, I believe that if I would have confessed Christ openly at that point, my time in the service would have been much more productive spiritually. People knew I had strong spiritual convictions—I wouldn't smoke, I wouldn't gamble, and so forth—and they just pretty much accepted me as I was, and I accepted them. They didn't give me a hard time about it. But I was never as vocal about my faith during the war as I should have been.

I spent the spring of 1944 in training. But D-Day, the great invasion of Europe by Allied Forces at Normandy, occurred on June 6, 1944. That was the exact day that I left Camp Grant on a train for the East Coast. I was going to join the war in Europe.

As the train rode through the mountains in Western Pennsylvania, I was struck by their beauty. I had never been in mountains before. We had some fairly good-sized hills in Michigan, but nothing compared to the mountains of Pennsylvania. I recalled the Scripture I had memorized as a child: "As the mountains surrounds Jerusalem, so the Lord surrounds his people." That verse got a hold of me, and as the train rolled through the Allegheny Mountains, I went out between the cars and stood on the railing, just bathing myself in that Scripture verse. I probably spent an hour out there, reminding myself that whatever happened to me I was in the Lord's hands. It made such an impression on me that I was never afraid in all the time I was in Europe for the war.

On my nineteenth birthday, July 27, 1944, I was on the troop ship and passed the Statue of Liberty, heading over to Bristol, England. While I was in England there was another young fellow that I hit it off with. We both liked to walk and explore things, so every chance we got, we'd go walking in the area, looking at all the big castles and as much as we could see. It was very different than what I'd grown up with in Union, Michigan. Whenever I could, I'd head into Bristol, where my brother-in-law, Harold Blough, was a medic. He showed me the famous Ashley Down orphanage that George Müller, a great evangelist during the nineteenth century, built. He cared for over ten thousand orphans during his lifetime, giving them a Christian education. It was very impressive.

The war effort was massive and complex. There was a whole system of depots and staging areas to send men and materials to the front. I spent six months in this replacement system, waiting for my turn to rotate into combat. I spent about eight weeks in England and was then moved forward toward the staging depots in France and Belgium, closer to the front lines.

The trip across the Channel was a tremendous experience. We got in a little English ship and headed over for what was supposed to be a short trip to France. But the sea was so rough that we couldn't unload. We spent three days out in the channel just bobbing around. Now fortunately, I didn't get sick either time that I was on the water, in crossing the Atlantic or the channel, but some of the guys got terribly seasick. For three days we had to take turns sleeping in hammocks, or just sleeping on our duffel bags. Rations were getting low, and all we had was greasy "Limey stew," the English beef stew.

After three days we landed at the same place where the biggest part of the D-Day invasion had taken place, Omaha Beach. By that time they'd built makeshift docks by sinking ships and pouring concrete over them. It was a nice dock for unloading. Then we got on boxcars. There were forty of us to a boxcar, but at least we didn't have the eight horses with us like they had in WWI. We were just forty men in the box, rolling across France and into Belgium, towards the forward staging depots. It was late fall, and the weather was turning wet.

These staging camps weren't bad. We were a few miles behind the front, and we slept in pup tents. But we had good chow, even though it rained a lot and we had to slop through the mud without galoshes to get to the chow line. At least we weren't getting sick or shot at like the guys at the front. I was content, knowing that I was in the Lord's hands and that he would determine the timing of whatever happened to me. Throughout my life, whenever I've gotten impatient or frustrated with God's timing, I've been surprised that He knew exactly what He was doing.

I went into combat on Thanksgiving Day, and my first action was going through the Siegfried Line. I was with the first troops that went into Germany through that line of advance. I was assigned to the 451st Medical Collecting company as a clerk typist. Our commanding officer, a captain, was a man of few morals and very hard to please. I wasn't too good of a clerk typist, so I had a sense that he would find another use for me. We had four-man teams that were assigned to be on the front line with the infantry. These teams were to collect the wounded and evacuate them to medical stations a short distance in the rear as quickly as possible. Our captain was unhappy with a man on one of these teams, and brought him back for permanent "KP duty"—serving in the kitchen, which was considered punishment. He put me on that team to replace this guy, and assigned a favorite of his to be his clerk-typist. I never saw the captain after that.

The day before Thanksgiving they moved my team forward. It was a hilly, deeply wooded region, and in late November it was getting cold. In fact, the winter of 1944 was the coldest winter Europe had had in a century. There weren't deep foxholes, but men had dug in as much as they could and stacked logs and branches in front of themselves to provide some cover. When my four-man team arrived, someone pointed us to one of these shallow holes with the logs in front, and we settled in to get some sleep.

The next day we had a good Thanksgiving dinner on the line, and the day after that the troops entered Germany through a series of defensive positions

Another photo from basic training.

the Nazi's called the Siegfried Line. There were big concrete pillboxes half-buried in the ground, with machine gun openings. Yankee ingenuity had come up with a solution to deal with them: men went forward the night before and put explosive charges on top of these bunkers. The next day, just before the infantry was ready to go in, they detonated these charges, and anyone who was in the pillbox was either killed or disoriented. With this tactic, our unit experienced no casualties going through the Siegfried Line.

I'll never forget that day. The first thing I saw on my first day in combat was a dead German soldier lying there. Somebody had gone through his pockets. He had a wallet with pictures of a wife and three or four kids. It hit me right off the bat, Hey, these people are family people just like us. They've been forced into this, so don't hate them as individuals. I knew the people at the top, the German leadership and the SS troops, were violent, wicked men. But there were a lot of regular guys who had just been drawn into this like we had been drawn into it. In our training we had been shown films about why we had to fight the war and defeat the Nazis, but right away this tempered me down and made me realize what war was all about.

So our goal, or my goal at least, and desire, was to do everything I could do to fight the men responsible for this war, to get rid of them, but also to help the common soldier. Ironically, with the fighting going well for our side at that point, most of the wounded my team brought back to the field hospital were German soldiers. In fact, we brought back so many wounded German prisoners that I ended up staying for eight months after the war ended working to help them recuperate and get released. In the end, I didn't have any internal moral struggle with the combat. I was able to accept it.

On the 16th of December, 1944, the Germans launched a massive counterattack that came to be known as the Battle of the Bulge, and I found myself right in the middle of it. We were attached directly to the 1st Army. Our orders were to accompany any 1st Army unit that was expecting heavy casualties and to evacuate the wounded as quickly as possible. We ended up falling back to defend ourselves in a small German castle. Our troops garrisoned inside, and there were German soldiers camped all around us. No one knew what was going to happen, but everyone knew that something was going to happen.

Our medical collection unit was brought up to spend the night with the infantry in this position. Once again, strangely enough, I was not afraid. I went to sleep and didn't worry about it. I think the other guys thought I was kind of crazy. Of course, they were all smoking out of nervousness, and I didn't smoke. The tension was pretty thick because we were outnumbered and our position wasn't too defendable. If the Germans had come straight ahead against us, we would have been in bad shape.

But instead, they went six or seven miles south along the Allied lines and broke through down there. The 1st Army really held the flank, and the main fighting was down around the Belgian town of Bastogne. The U.S. Airborne's defense of Bastogne became one of the most famous battles of the war. They took a tremendous beating, but held. General Patton rushed up and relieved them, and my unit was put with a field hospital. We helped take care of the wounded from the Battle of the Bulge. A lot of them were sent to our outfit, and we helped patch them up, get them onto planes, and sent back to England. One of the hardest parts of that was there were kids who had just shipped out of the States earlier that week who had been sent directly to the front to respond to the German attack. We were sending them back a week later, wounded. There were a lot of wounded. I did attempt to share my faith with some who were in bad shape physically. I can't really say that I led anybody to the Lord, but I prayed with some.

The Battle of the Bulge lasted five weeks. By that time, Allied forces were able to reorient and respond to the German advance. It really was a last, desperate attack by Hitler, and when it sputtered, it was the beginning of the end for the Nazis. The last night of the battle, the night that German units that had been surrounded began to surrender, we were called with our unit to go out into the field. We picked up seven wounded German soldiers and loaded them onto our Jeep to take them to the hospital.

But the war wasn't over. The Allies had to drive to Berlin to end it, and to do that they first had to cross the Rur River and then the Rhine River. The next objective was a large dam on the river that had to be taken. The Canadians and British were at the river, and two units advanced into the town on the Western bank, but they didn't dare cross for fear that the Germans would blow the dam. That would have been a disaster for all the units, not to mention towns, below it. The advance units were pulled out of the town, and the army was held up, waiting for instructions from headquarters.

The road down to the town and the dam hadn't been cleared of German land mines. We were on the top of a hill on the western side of the river, overlooking the town and the dam. The Germans had artillery on

A German 88mm cannon, one of the most famous weapons of the war.

the hills on the other side. Eventually, forward units were given the order to take the dam, regardless of casualties. Our medical collection unit would have to follow the infantry to evacuate the wounded we all knew were inevitable.

So we got into a tracked vehicle called a Weasel. It was small and light, like a Jeep, so it didn't offer a lot of protection. The driver told us to get down as low as we could and hang on, and he took off, zigzagging down this hill, going toward a small town. Artillery shells were landing around us, and at least three came pretty close to our vehicle. It appeared that the German artillery battery had seen our Weasel and were aiming directly at it. That was surprising, since we had the red cross painted on it. The Germans generally respected medical units and rarely aimed fire at them.

But this day, this battery did. It was probably an "88," the German 88mm cannon that was one of the most famous weapons of the war. We kept our heads down, and the driver zigged and zagged through the incoming fire going down that hill. We made it into the edge of the little town. A group of American soldiers were there, and as we were coming up there a shell landed very close to us. One man took shrapnel in his leg. I was about as close to the impact as he was, but nothing hit me.

We were told to find a house and sleep for the night, so at random we picked out a house and settled down in it to sleep. Of course, the other three guys in my unit smoked like fiends. I have always felt that if the Germans had snuck back to that town in the night they could have found us in that house just by the smell of all that smoke. We woke up at dawn with a tremendous urge to just get out of there. We got in our vehicle, went to another part of town, and had our rations. An hour later we came back to find that there had been a direct artillery hit on that house. It was completely demolished. If we hadn't gotten out of there, there was no way we would have survived.

That night the Allies decided they had to capture the dam. The infantry went in, and as they approached it through the town the Germans let loose a tremendous barrage. Two men were wounded at the first building, and two more went down a short distance away. My unit was ordered to come forward and pick up the wounded. When we got up to the road leading down the hill to the dam, the Jeep driver stopped and said he wouldn't go down any further because the road hadn't been cleared of mines. He was insistent.

I said we had to go because there were wounded men down there, and it was our duty to evacuate them. I was the youngest and lowest-ranked man in the group, and I shouldn't have been arguing with him at all. But I said, "Guys, we've gotta go down." The driver repeated himself, saying he wouldn't go forward. After about ten or fifteen minutes of this bickering, I put my foot down. I told the others that we were going down that road to get the wounded, and that I'd walk ahead of the Jeep to check for buried mines.

And I did. I started walking down the road, and they followed a short distance behind me, careful to drive where I had walked. We got down to the first building and collected the first two casualties. The officer in charge said there were guys further down the way who were wounded worse than those, and asked if we would go forward and get them. So I started out again, walking ahead of the the Jeep. We got down about halfway to where the next wounded soldiers were, and shots rang out around us. We dove for the ditch. But I said we needed to keep moving forward. One of the guys said, "Go ahead, you d— fool! Get yourself killed if you want to, but I'm going back." He and the other two guys in my collection team turned around and went back to the first building. When they got there the officer in charge said that since we'd opened up the road by showing it wasn't mined, his men could bring the wounded who were near the front line out, and that we could take the first two wounded men back to the hospital.

I was always thankful that I didn't chicken out that day. It was my job to rescue those wounded men, and with the help of the Lord I was able to do it. It's been a great satisfaction in my life. Napoleon once said, "If I can control myself I can control an army." I found out that day that I could control myself. Because I could face the music, so to speak, the other guys followed me. It was a tremendous lesson: If I can control myself, I can control an army. I've been reminded of that so many times since then, and it's given me the courage to lead others in business and ministry. I've been able to share it with others and help them become better leaders. If we can lead ourselves, by the help of the Lord, we can lead others to serve Jesus Christ.

During that time I wrote a different kind of letter home. Our outgoing mail was censored by the army to make sure we didn't give away any secrets about our position or plans. We couldn't say anything about where we were. But I was able to use a little code and write to my parents, trying to tell them I was in Germany and where I was. There had been a farm not far from ours that was owned by a family named Wagner. The farm was sold to another family from Chicago, whose last name was Schmitt—they were of German descent. In my letter, I said that I had met the people who had bought the old Wagner farm. I found out later that, even before my letter arrived, my father felt a strong burden to spend time alone in prayer for my protection and safety. When they received the letter, it confirmed that the days he felt the burden to pray were the exact days I was in great danger! I feel that to a great extent I owe my survival to my father's prayers and intercession.

After we crossed the Rhine, the difficult fighting was over. The Germans lost a lot of people and equipment, and by then the Russians were closing in on Berlin from the east. My unit was with the first troops to cross the famous bridge at Remagen, the one that didn't get blown up. We were advancing with the first infantry troops, and we ended up at a German air base about a hundred miles from Berlin. We stayed there until the Russians took Berlin and Hitler killed himself. The war was over.

Of course, there were tremendous celebrations. There was wine by the flagon—water cans full of wine. I didn't drink the wine, but I joined in the celebration. It was great that the war was over, but I knew enough about the situation to realize that they were preparing for the invasion of Japan. My brother was in a unit that was all ready to go, and since I had low seniority points, I was really expecting that I would be sent to organize another medical unit and be involved in the invasion of Japan.

In the end, I was kept in Germany eight more months to help wounded German prisoners of war get well enough to be sent back home. In March of 1946 I came back on one of those little victory ships. Crossing the North Atlantic in March was rough, but, thankfully, I did not get seasick. I was sent to Camp McCoy in Wisconsin, and was mustered out of the military there. It was time to go home.

WAR REFLECTION

A photo of me in uniform.

"As the mountains surround Jerusalem, so the Lord surrounds his people both now and forevermore."

Psalm 125:2

"Whoever acknowledges me before others, I will also acknowledge before my Father in heaven. But whoever disowns me before others, I will disown before my Father in heaven."

Matthew 10:32-33

When I had entered the army and was on the train going east, Psalm 125:2 came to me. I knew that I was in the Lord's hands no matter what, and this kept me from being afraid during the war.

But Matthew 10:32-33 also applied to me during the war. I failed to kneel by my bunk and pray that first night. I still can't understand why, because I sat there for a long time trying to work up the courage to do it in front of the other guys. Because of this I went through my whole service career without the spiritual victory I should have had. Jesus could not give it to me because I had denied him.

A HAUNTING EXPERIENCE

"Do not store up for yourselves treasures on earth, where moths and vermin destroy, and where thieves break in and steal. But store up for yourselves treasures in heaven, where moths and vermin do not destroy, and where thieves do not break in and steal."

Matthew 6:19-20

I want to share something from my army experience that has come back to my mind probably more often than any other, sometimes with a very positive effect, but more often in a haunting way. One of the houses I went into during combat had German money scattered all over the floor of one of the rooms. The picture is so vivid in my mind. There was still a little of it in a drawer; I suppose that all of the money had been in that drawer and one of the soldiers who had been there before me had scattered it over the floor. The thing that impressed me was that a family at one time had placed considerable value on that money, but now it was completely worthless. When they had to leave the house, there was no need to take it with them.

I know this helped me when I felt the Lord ask me to give up $500, half of my new car money, to help a young missionary after the war. It also helped me make the decision to give up my half share of a prospering business to pastor a church that paid $25 a week. This experience encouraged me all through my life to be content in making just enough to support the family with a little left over.

The haunting, fearful part of seeing this worthless money scattered and left behind as a family runs for their lives is that it could so easily happen to any of us, in a literal or figurative sense. We are people consumed by and in love with so much other than the riches of Christ and His Word. In our day, political correctness seeks to silence the Truth of the joy and blessing found in a life lived in and for Christ. We are left with worthless treasures that will not bring meaningful life here or eternal life in heaven.

I pray that this haunting experience of mine will encourage you to seek Christ and the riches found in Him. "Oh the depths of the riches of the wisdom and knowledge of God" (Romans 11:33).

MY DEAR WIFE'S FAMILY

Thomas and Laura Byers

Norma Jean's family has enriched my life immensely. They are the Byers family from Pennsylvania. Benjamin Franklin Byers was born in 1837 and served in the Civil War. He then settled down to farm on a 160-acre farm that was an original land grant from William Penn. It was called Roseland and was a postal stop during the 1800s. The farm was kept in the family for many years, but Benjamin moved with his family to Coalport, PA, in the late 1800s.

One of his sons, Thomas, fell in love with and married a lovely, serious-minded young lady named Laura Thompson. Her father had been part of the cavalry during the Civil War and distinguished himself by being chosen to stand as one of the Honor Guards when President Lincoln's body was lying in state in Harrisburg, PA. Laura loved the Lord with all her heart and shared her faith with many in the town of Coalport. Soon, a group of believers were meeting regularly in Thomas and Laura's living room. It grew until finally Laura convinced Thomas' brother Sam, the owner of the General Store, to build them a church.

Thomas and Laura would often take the train to New York City and listen to A. B. Simpson, a Presbyterian minister and founder of the Christian and Missionary Alliance. Rev. Simpson had a passion and burden for worldwide missions. Thomas and Laura felt God's call and began to prepare for overseas missions. Before they got started in their training, however, a scandal in their home church put an end to their plans. The pastor and organist had an affair and left town together. Thomas was disappointed and disillusioned and stated, "If this is how Christians act, I want nothing to do with them!" It was not until later in his seventies that he regretted the wasted time and again actively supported the work of Christ.

Laura was devastated with this turn of events, and this, together with the tragic death of one of their young sons, caused a severe depression. Thomas had to hire a housekeeper to help keep the home functioning. While this was a very dark time in her life, Laura continued to seek the Lord and fought her way back. She became a tremendous witness for Christ once again, started another church in her living room, and helped many, many women in times of spiritual need. Later on, she was a great encouragement to Norma Jean when our first baby was stillborn.

Thomas and Laura had six children, one of whom was Donald, Norma Jean's father. He was born in 1902 and lived most of his childhood in Coalport, PA. Donald developed an early interest in and talent for sales. He sold little gadgets to the local people, and even got the agency for Fleischman's yeast. One of the happiest days of his life was when he had enough money to buy a new Columbia bicycle for $17. He then expanded his route and made even more money.

By the time Donald was a teenager, his family had moved to Youngstown, OH. Donald took an after-school job in a garage, and while on the job he happened to be at the wrong place at the wrong time. A tire explosion caused a severe eye injury. After many treatments and surgeries his eye healed, but the accident had prevented him from graduating with his classmates. Rather than finish his high school education with younger students, he moved by himself to Valparaiso, IN, and finished there.

Donald's ambitions were high, and he saw a profession in sales as his ticket to success. He headed to Chicago, hoping to find employment with the prosperous Kirk Soap Company, the largest manufacture of soap in the United States. One day, standing near the loading docks behind the factory on North Water Street, Donald struck up a conversation with a gentleman there, mentioning that he would love the opportunity to work at the company. The gentleman surprised Donald by telling him to present himself to the front office. When he did, he realized that the man on the loading dock had been none other than the owner, Mr. Kirk himself! Mr. Kirk really liked Donald, and he not only hired him, but also gave him $100 to go downtown and buy a new suit.

Donald worked for Kirk Soap for a while, learned a lot about business, and then decided he wanted to go to Wharton School of Business at the University

Donald Byers, twenty years old.

Mae Rodgers, twenty years old.

of Pennsylvania. Not knowing that he needed to apply and be accepted, he just drove to Philadelphia and showed up at the campus. They asked if he was registered, and he replied that he did not know anything about that, but he was there to attend the school! They took him on probation.

It was during this time that he met Mae Rodgers. Mae was the youngest daughter of Andrew and Martha Rodgers. Martha's father, John R. Rhoads, fought in the battle of Gettysburg and also invented the railroad turnstile. Donald was just helping a friend who couldn't keep a date with Mae, but when he met her, it was love at first sight. He said to himself, "There she is. There's my wife!" They were married in December of 1925.

Donald completed one year at Wharton, but he was anxious to start making money. It was 1926 and things were booming everywhere, but especially in California. Donald wasn't the only one in his family wanting adventure, so in the summer of 1926, Donald and Mae, Thomas and Laura (Grandma and Grandpa Byers), and Donald's brother and sister, Paul and Ruth, all traveled in a touring car from Youngstown, OH, to San Diego, CA. The roads were very rough. Grandpa insisted they travel only two hundred miles a day. They cooked all their own meals and spent the nights in tourist cabins, which required that they provide their own bedding. With perseverance they finally made it safely and with no great difficulty. Once in California they were able to rent a lovely furnished house with plenty of room for the whole family.

Donald began working for an insurance company and did extremely well. He started buying used cars and selling them to sailors. He made a profit on the cars and the insurance for them as well. At Wharton, he had been taught to borrow money and invest it in the stock market. Donald did this and was making money. His hopes of becoming a millionaire looked promising. He even had a nice spot picked out in the mountains where he would build his big house. In the

midst of this exciting, promising time, in November of 1927, Norma Jean was born. Donald and Mae were very happy and proud of their daughter.

While the family was living in San Diego, Grandma Byers started attending a Christian and Missionary Alliance church that was pastored by a retired missionary. Pastor Quick was a godly man and very personable. Mae attended with Grandma Byers, and it wasn't long before Mae believed in the message of Christ's love and salvation and decided to follow Him. Mae, Grandma Byers, and even little Norma Jean began praying that Donald would also give his life to Christ. Earlier in his life Donald had felt a strong call to become a minister, but now had no time for spiritual things.

It is not hard to imagine the tension there must have been at times. The men had no interest in spiritual things and were mainly thinking about making money. The women were very involved in their church and were praying earnestly for their husbands and sons to find and follow Christ. This all came to a head one day when Donald came home from work to find his brother Paul angrily throwing his clothes into a suitcase. When asked what he was doing, Paul replied, "Lord, Lord, all I ever hear around here is 'The Lord this and The Lord that!' I am getting out of here." He took off and drove straight back to Youngstown.

The year 1929 came, and the Great Depression affected Donald and the family drastically. Donald lost everything when the stock market crashed. He lost the money he had borrowed as well. He refused to take bankruptcy and determined that he would pay back all the money he had borrowed. He had some money in the bank, but all the banks closed, so he lost that as well. The bank would not apply his money toward what he had borrowed, so he had to work until 1939 to pay off his debts.

As with many families during the Great Depression, Donald and his little family tried but could not make it on their own. In 1932 they moved in with his parents. Grandma and Grandpa Byers were back in Youngstown, OH, now and made them feel welcome, but the house at 42 S. Whitney was small—only three bedrooms—and Donald, Mae, and Norma Jean weren't the only ones who needed a place to stay. Eight adults and one child shared the home. Norma Jean and her parents had a fairly good-sized bedroom upstairs, but very limited kitchen facilities and access only to one bathroom shared by all. Uncle Paul slept on a small enclosed porch. Aunt Ruth had the other upstairs room as her bedroom by night, but it became a living room by day. Grandma and Grandpa had their bedroom downstairs. The shared bathroom was off the hall just outside their bedroom, but this hall was where Virginia, a teenage relative, slept. Great-grandma Thompson slept and lived in the living/dining room area, and the dog slept in the kitchen! These living arrangements continued until Norma Jean's family moved to Pittsburg, PA, in 1935.

Despite the cramped conditions, Norma Jean has pleasant memories of that time. She spent time reading to her great-grandma and helping her with scrapbooks. Great-grandma Thompson encouraged her to learn to play the piano. Norma Jean grew to dearly love her Grandma Byers. She was a very godly influence in her life and a powerful role model. Her motto was "Consistency, thou art a jewel!" Grandma Byers kept the household running smoothly, and she was a saint if there ever was one. She would not come out of her bedroom in the morning until she had her personal devotions. After they all had daily family prayer time, she would say, "Now we are covered!"

Grandma, Mae, and Norma Jean consistently prayed for Donald to truly commit himself to Christ. Years went by, and events kept happening that drew Donald to Christ. One time, a minister asked Donald if he was now willing to make a commitment. Donald again refused. The minister wisely said, "Donald, would you be willing to be made willing?" He was honestly able to answer, "Yes, I am willing to be made willing."

The most outstanding event that changed his life, however, was a very serious automobile accident. Donald and a young trainee were headed to a restaurant at the end of a long day. Both had had a few drinks at the hotel bar, and it was a dark, rainy evening. While driving on a gravel road Donald swerved too sharply, and the car went sailing over the embankment, over a fence, and landed in a wet, grassy bog. The steering wheel broke off in his hands, but worst of all, he couldn't find the young man. He realized he was in deep trouble. Then and there, he promised to serve the Lord if he got out of this mess.

Mae, Donald, and Norma Jean, 1928.

Shortly thereafter he found the young man, knocked out and thrown up under the cowl of the car. Though he had a very serious bump on his head, he did survive. They agreed to keep the accident a secret, and Donald even replaced the car with the exact model and color so he wouldn't have to tell Mae what had happened. He did keep his promise, though, and about a year later, at the age of forty, he committed the remainder of his life to serving the Lord.

Donald made drastic changes. He sold nearly everything they owned and moved the whole family to Nyack, NY. They had eighty dollars and their few belongings in their suitcases. Donald attended the C&MA Missionary Training Institute and prepared to go into full-time ministry. He was finally obedient to the calling God had given him earlier in his life to preach the Gospel.

One prayer had been answered, and soon another would be answered. Norma Jean had been praying long and hard for a baby sister. A baby brother, Donny, had joined the family when Norma Jean was twelve. She loved him and enjoyed helping to care for him. At Nyack, however, when Norma Jean was seventeen years old, her mother had another baby. Laura Lee, her sweet baby sister, was born. Less than a year later, Norma Jean left home to start at Ft. Wayne Bible Institute.

Left: Norma Jean and Laura Lee.
Right: Baby Donny and Norma Jean.

SCRABBLE

Norma Jean has been a Scrabble fan for many years. She especially liked to play with the grandchildren. They really had some good games. It was fun for me just to watch the excitement of their games.

Our son-in-law Stan Gerig, Cindy's husband, is full of creative ideas. For Norma Jean's eightieth birthday, he decided to take an extra Scrabble board that they had and make this decorative piece. Do you want to see what words you can find?

Explanation: FAIR LADY. FT WAYNE (where we met at Bible school). GLENNS LITTLE BYERS GIRL. NORMA GENIUS (what we called her sometimes). MARKS XO (hugs and kisses). EIGHTIETH BDAY.

OUR COLLEGE YEARS

The war was over, I had been mustered out of the army at Camp McCoy, Wisconsin, and I returned home. During the four months I was home before going back to Fort Wayne Bible Institute, I realized and admitted what a flop my spiritual life had been during the war. The words of the song, "Marvelous grace of our loving Lord, grace that exceeds our sin and our guilt" became a reality in my heart and life. But I was still a very beaten and confused young man. The war was very much a part of me. The last thing on my mind was a girlfriend, but the Lord must have had a different idea.

The night of freshman orientation at Fort Wayne, I walked into the large meeting room and saw that there was a whole row of girls sitting on one side of the room, but there wasn't a single guy in there yet. I went in and sat down about in the middle of an empty row. Then my whole life of enjoying being a loner suddenly left me, and I got up and sat in an empty chair that was on the side of the girls. It happened to be right beside Norma Jean. I just got up, walked across the room, and sat down in this empty chair, which was so unlike me. I said to her, "I just decided there was no need for me to be sitting there by myself." We got acquainted a little bit that night.

Soon after that, one of the professors was taking flying lessons and the plane crashed. The pilot was killed and the professor was injured and in the hospital. Since I had been a medic in the army, I offered to relieve his wife and stay with him in the hospital. Well, I missed my assignments. I knew Norma Jean was an exceptionally good student, so I asked her what assignments I missed. It was a good excuse to spend some time with her.

We were assigned seats at family-style tables during the week, but during the weekend we could sit wherever we wanted. Of course, the first semester they wouldn't allow any dating at all, but we could sit together on weekends. So Norma Jean and I started sitting together. We saw that we had some things in common. She sensed that I was serious, and I sensed that she was serious. I finally got the courage to ask her if she would go to a missionary film with me on a Friday night on the campus. She said, "Sure, I wanted to go anyway," and that was

Norma Jean and I at Fort Wayne Bible Institute.

our first date, on December 6, 1946. From that time on we just seemed to be pretty much committed to each other.

It has always been a marvel to me that as messed up as I had been, and as unsure of myself as I was, still my Heavenly Father brought me into contact with one of the most spiritual, most dedicated girls on the whole campus. An even greater miracle was that she thought I was one of the most spiritual and dedicated guys on campus. "Love is blind," as the old saying goes, but the cleansing blood and the mighty power of Jesus Christ had changed me and was changing me more and more. Thank you Jesus!

• • •

I could have drawn unemployment for a while after I got back from Europe, but I didn't care for that. I did for maybe a couple of weeks, and then I found a job with my Uncle Clayton pouring concrete. My brother Don came back about the same time as me, so we both went to work with him. It was hard work, but we had both recently gotten out of the army, so we were in good health and had a lot of energy. I set to work, continuing even after I restarted Bible school.

Uncle Clayton was a top-notch concrete finisher. He boasted of the fact that he went from Goshen to Warsaw in a pair of boots, pouring the concrete road. He taught us that "You work the concrete or it will work you." That is true of a lot of things. If you really get at a task and get it done, it's a lot easier than if you neglect or just putter around with it. Don and I both became quite skilled at handling concrete.

One day Maynard Yoder, the head of Redi-Mix Concrete Co., came and said, "You guys are getting along pretty good. Would you be interested in another job?" They were building prefab homes that needed concrete foundations. The five guys they had were having a lot of trouble getting two foundations done a week. Somehow Maynard thought we might be interested and could handle that. Our dad told us,

"Boys, don't take anything on contract—you'll lose your shirt." But we took putting in those foundations on contract, and we got the same amount as the other guys were getting. Before very long we worked it out that with one more man we could put in a foundation a day, and that's how we were making money.

In 1948, when we started up our own business, we needed some materials to make forms. We went to Newman Munger lumber company in Elkhart and talked to the manager, and it ended up that we needed to buy about $500 worth of material. We were a couple of kids who had just gotten out of the army, but he looked at us and said, "Are you Johnny Marks' grandchildren?" We said yes, and he said, "If you're Johnny Marks' grandsons, you can charge anything you want." Talk about family connections! Grandpa Marks had that reputation. We bought that material, fixed up a set of forms, bought a tractor, and we were ready to go. We put in foundations in Elkhart, and it was close by. My brother Don was really the leader of the business, and I worked along with him and supported him. At this time I was also in college. During my senior year I worked and took eighteen credit hours both semesters. By 1949 we were making $100 a day. That was good money, the equivalent of more than $800 in today's money. I'm sure I made more money than the college president!

• • •

While in the army I sent practically all of my money home to save up to buy a new car. I hadn't had a car before, and I wanted one. When I got home I had enough money, but when I went to the dealer in Cassopolis, no cars were available because there weren't enough in production. There was a long waiting list. So I had this money in the bank, and there was a young lady named Betty in the church who wanted to go to Africa as a missionary. The Lord said to me, pull your money out and put it in the Lord's work. And I was able to do it. I pulled every cent out and said, "Alright Lord, what do you want me to do with it?"

Well, I gave $100 to one project, and then the Lord spoke to me very definitely: Give Betty $500. That was half of my money gone. I had no idea what she needed, but years later she came to me and said, "Glenn, did you know how much money I needed to get ready for the mission field?" I said no, and she said, "The $500 you gave me was just what I needed." I learned that money is alright, but it's not the most important thing. But the Lord gave me a new car when I really needed it, and I was able to write out a check to pay for it.

• • •

I never have really understood what my problem was, but I seemed unable to concentrate and complete all of my assignments at Fort Wayne. I flunked two classes, messing up my GI Bill eligibility. Then, during the summer a recruiter convinced me to transfer to Bethel College. Bethel was our own denomination's school, and it was just opening in 1947, so I was among its first students. By this time I had thoroughly made up my mind to get back on track with my college work. I did the first semester at Bethel without the GI Bill. Things went well, and I was able to get back on it. At that time the Bible course they were offering was acceptable for going into the ministry, so I never went to seminary.

Norma Jean was not happy about me changing schools, and she didn't come to Bethel the first semester. Instead, she stayed home in Ohio. I was still working when I could. I would go to class during the day and pour concrete in the afternoons. I spent quite a bit of time working hard, but I also took off to go see Norma Jean. I would drive down on every vacation, even though I could make $100 a day if I didn't. Again, I had learned that money was not the most important thing in the world.

Norma Jean came to Bethel my second semester, and our romance continued. During the summer of 1948 I was able to go to Norma Jean's parents' for a visit, and that went very well. Also that summer,

Norma Jean was serving tables at Beulah Beach, the Christian and Missionary Alliance campground. I was able to attend there, and we were both baptized in Lake Erie.

We were both taking Bible, general ed, and

Another photo of Norma Jean and I, this time at Bethel College.

ministry classes, and our thoughts about the future were centered on foreign missionary work. Norma Jean grew up in the Christian Missionary Alliance, and they were strong on missions and had a very organized program.

Norma Jean and I began to think very seriously about getting married. My proposal was really romantic. I said, "As far as I am concerned, I think that you are the one I would like to be my wife." It took her a while to respond, but she agreed. At the time the college was permitting married students to set up a mobile home on campus, as we were going to do that. But we postponed our wedding plans at the urging of my brother and Norma Jean's dad.

Norma Jean graduated from a two-year Bible course in 1949, and she did not come back to school in the fall. Her father was now the director of a Jewish mission in New York City, and the family had moved there. Norma Jean took a position as a nanny for a wealthy family living on Long Island, and she was treated very well in the home. I was alone at Bethel and very lonely. I drove to New York and spent Christmas with the Byers family, and this went very well. I bought her a very nice "hope chest," and we made some wedding plans. Norma Jean still had some doubts, but one day her mother talked to her and said, "Norma Jean, you will have to do what you have to do, but I will tell you this: you will go a long way before you find another young man as nice as Glenn Marks."

Soon after that, Norma Jean got peace of mind and heart about our marriage. We decided on June 8, as soon as possible after graduation from Bethel. We decided to get married in Nyack, New York, with Rev. Harold Freligh performing the ceremony. He was a very close family friend and the most spiritual person we knew.

As graduation drew close, we checked with the mission board, and they said, "Sorry, right after the war we filled up all of the spots. We have people ready to go out, and we're not sending any more missionaries right now." We were not going to be accepted on the foreign field, even though that's what both of us wanted. I was tempted, and I became hesitant about leaving a $100 a day income. I suggested to Norma Jean that maybe I should remain in the business and send a lot of money to missionaries. She looked at me and fired back her answer: "I promised to marry a preacher, not a builder. Stay in the business if you want to, but count me out." That was all I needed to help me decide to turn the business over to my brother. I have never regretted my decision.

We didn't quite know what we were going to do, but we had a tremendously active, visionary Church Extension Director, Joe Kimble, and he was starting new churches throughout Indiana. He said to us, "Glenn and Norma Jean, why don't you go into home missions and enlarge the base? There's a closed church down in Plymouth, Indiana, and I've met with 'em. We've got a few people who are willing to work to open that church, and we think you and Norma Jean would really fit in well there."

So we accepted the challenge. After graduation and our wedding, we were ready to go to work planting and building churches.

IT COULDN'T BE DONE

Somebody said that it couldn't be done,
    But, he with a chuckle replied
That "maybe it couldn't," but he would be one
    Who wouldn't say so till he'd tried.
So he buckled right in with the trace of a grin
    On his face. If he worried he hid it.
He started to sing as he tackled the thing
    That couldn't be done, and he did it.

    Somebody scoffed: "Oh, you'll never do that;
        At least no one has done it";
    But he took off his coat and he took off his hat,
        And the first thing we knew he'd begun it.
    With a lift of his chin and a bit of a grin,
        Without any doubting or quiddit,
    He started to sing as he tackled the thing
        That couldn't be done, and he did it.

        There are thousands to tell you it cannot be done,
           There are thousands to prophesy failure;
        There are thousands to point out to you one by one,
           The dangers that wait to assail you.
        But just buckle it in with a bit of a grin,
           Just take off your coat and go to it;
        Just start to sing as you tackle the thing
           That "couldn't be done," and you'll do it.

Edgar Albert Guest

FORT WAYNE REFLECTION

> *"But seek first his kingdom and his righteousness, and all these things will be given to you as well."*
>
> Matthew 6:33

When I got back from the war I was confused and beat up. Memories of the wounded and dying soldiers, and of my own spiritual failures, were unbearable at times. The song "Grace Greater than Our Sin" became a favorite song of mine, and it still is today. I was in need of that "Marvelous grace of our loving Lord, grace that exceeds our sin and our guilt!" Matthew 6:33 was also important to me. I really got serious about spiritual things, finding again the Lord's forgiveness and peace. I was seeking first the kingdom of God, and he met me. I began to get things put together again.

At this time I went back to Fort Wayne Bible Institute, where I had been before the war, and there I met Norma Jean. It's such a miracle how God brought us together. I saw Norma Jean as one of the most spiritual and dedicated ladies in the school, and she had that same opinion of me. We just gravitated to each other. She was a challenge to me, and apparently I was a challenge to her.

Norma Jean had a tremendous influence on me, helping me get the war and army life out of my mind at a time when I was still very much subject to it. For example, I was in the library one day and somebody dropped a book on a table. The sound startled me, and before I knew what was happening, I was under the table. But as our friendship and romance grew, the war memories had less of a hold on me.

At Fort Wayne one of the professors taught us the song "A Charge to Keep I Have":

A charge to keep I have,
a God to glorify,
a never-dying soul to save,
and fit it for the sky.

To serve the present age,
my calling to fulfill;
O may it all my powers engage
to do my Master's will!

This challenge was probably one of the bigger things I learned during that year at Fort Wayne. It began to give me a sense of duty, purpose, and responsibility. Fort Wayne Bible Institute was great at teaching spiritual dedication and purpose in life, and I am grateful for my time there.

BETHEL REFLECTION

While at Prairie Camp, a family camp for our denomination, during the summer of 1948, a recruiter for Bethel College, which opened that year, talked me into transferring. I signed up and then told Norma Jean about it. She wasn't too happy about that, and she didn't come the first semester. I had trouble that year at Fort Wayne. I can't really explain it, but I couldn't get my work done. In fact, I flunked two courses at Fort Wayne. I would try to study and complete my work, but it wasn't happening. I messed up my GI Bill, and I admit I was a confused kid. But the summer before I went to Bethel I said, "Glenn, get a hold of yourself. You've got to get back in the groove." That first semester I worked very hard. I got good grades and got reinstated on the GI Bill. I ended up getting through college with a cum laude, a B average. Norma Jean was always summa cum laude.

While I was working at Bethel I took a job as a night watchman, working from midnight to seven o'clock in the morning. That was going fairly well, since I could study on the job and get my schoolwork done. The man whose office I worked in started putting up pornography on the wall, and I wanted nothing to do with it. I wrote a note that said, "If you're going to continue this, I'm going to have to quit." Of course, he didn't take it down, so I turned in my resignation. It wasn't too long after that when my brother and I started in business making $100 a day.

Norma Jean and I thought we might get married while we were in school. The college was allowing mobile homes on the campus at that time. We picked out a spot and a mobile home, we had financing from my father, and we were moving forward with our plans. However, her father and my brother really put the pressure on us, saying that we'd better finish college before we got married, so we gave that whole thing up. We had sense enough to honor parental advice, and it was the right decision, no question about it. The Lord watched over us in a lot of ways, and it was a wise decision.

One of our Bible teachers, S.I. Emery, had been a commissioned officer in World War I, as well as a tremendous, self-taught minister. He knew the Bible backwards and forwards. It was said that he and two other men could reproduce the entire Bible by memory. He was a great teacher and inspired the ministerial students with powerful illustrations. He believed strongly that hearing the Gospel, more than reading or observing, is what moves the soul spiritually. He was a true man of God, and his life and words made a lasting impression on Norma Jean and me.

THE GARDENER

"I am the true vine, and my Father is the gardener."

John 15:1

"I am the vine; you are the branches."

John 15:5

These words blessed my heart when they first caught my attention, and they continue to bless and challenge me. Very early in life I began helping my mother in our huge garden. I was probably about six when I started riding our horse and driving her between the rows while Daddy cultivated the garden. Most of our married life Norma Jean and I had large gardens. I have never considered myself a professional, but our gardens flourished and provided an abundance of vegetables for us and extra to share with neighbors and friends.

I have been searching the Scriptures to see what they say the Gardener does. The parable Jesus tells in Luke 13:6-9 says the gardener will "dig around it and fertilize it." John 15:2 says, "He cuts off every branch in me that bears no fruit, while every branch that does bear fruit he prunes so that it will be even more fruitful."

• Dig around: The gardener loosens the soil so the rain can soak in and weeds will not grow. Our Father works in our hearts and minds so we can receive Him and His Word (Philippians 1:6).

• Put on fertilizer: The gardener feeds the plants with what they need to produce fruit. Our Father feeds us with the Bread of Life (John 6:35).

• Prune: The gardener cuts away any dead, unnecessary, or hindering foliage so that more fruit will be produced. The Father removes anything that prevents a fruitful life (John 15:2).

If your heart's desire is to let the Heavenly Father be the Gardener of your life and be fruitful for Christ, then consider this verse: "I am the vine; you are the branches. If you remain in me and I in you, you will bear much fruit; apart from me you can do nothing" (John 15:5). You can "remain in Christ" by living in the Word and setting your will to do God's will. Our Heavenly Father can then be the Gardener of your heart and life.

OUR WEDDING

We were married on June 8, 1950, in the Old Stone Church in Nyack, New York. The ceremony, reception, and decorations were all quite simple, but we were happy to celebrate the day with our families and friends.

The church was built in 1830, and since there was no organ, we loaded up the old Byers pump organ and brought that to the church. Norma Jean really wanted an arbor decorated with real flowers. I built the arbor for my bride and climbed the locust trees to get enough flowers to cover the arbor.

Afterwards, we took a ten-day honeymoon throughout all of the New England states. We stayed in little cabins that cost only about $5 a night. It was a great trip, but for one thing. About three days into the trip, I was covered with poison oak! I must have gotten it climbing the locust trees.

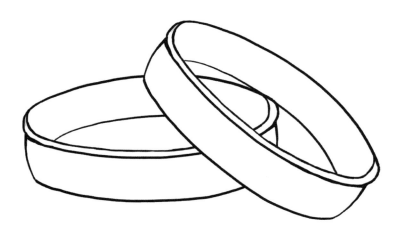

Norma Jean and I on our wedding day in 1950.

MY WONDERFUL WIFE AND HELPER

"A good woman is hard to find, and worth far more than diamonds."

Proverbs 31:10

Norma Jean was born in San Diego, California, on November 21, 1927. Her parents had recently moved there, believing this was the place to get rich quick and make her father's dreams of becoming a millionaire come true.

Norma Jean was a bright and energetic child, always eager to learn. Her mother loved to sing and taught her daughter many songs. As a tiny child, her father would bring her to work, stand her up on his desk, and let her "sing her songs" for his colleagues at the office.

Norma Jean was not afraid to speak her mind, even at a young age. At times this was humorous, such as when she was supposed to sing "Brighten the Corner" at church. When she got up front, she announced, "I know a better song: 'Trust and Obey.'" She sang that instead.

During another performance, Norma Jean was encouraged by the director to bow before starting to sing. From center stage, Norma Jean put her hands on her hips, turned to the director, who was off stage, and said, "My mother said I should bow after, and you say I should bow before. Now I don't know what to do!" The audience, especially her uncle, got a good laugh.

Other times, however, speaking her mind got her in trouble, and her mother disciplined her by making her sit on a chair. During one of these "time outs," Norma Jean fussed and squirmed on the chair until she finally called to her mother, "Mother, I can't get comforter!" Her mother replied, "I don't want you to get 'comforter.' I want you to know why you are sitting there!"

Norma Jean, 1947.

The Great Depression had taken away her father's hopes of becoming a millionaire. He became a traveling salesman, and for much of Norma Jean's formative years, the family moved very often. She was in a different school almost every year, but she still was able to keep her grades very high. She was able to skip one year of elementary school and graduated very near the top of her large high school class in Nyack, New York.

When she was a senior in high school she entered the Westinghouse Talent Search and was runner-up for the state of New York. Her academic strengths were math and science. Because of her high score on the Westinghouse Talent Search, she was offered many college scholarships at prestigious universities. As a high school senior she was working at Letterly Laboratories and was immediately noticed by the head chemist, who moved her from an entry-level job to one with more responsibility. She could have had a career in the secular world, especially as a woman in the growing field of chemical engineering.

However, she gave it all up because she wanted to go to Bible school and find a place of service for Jesus. Norma Jean had never heard of Fort Wayne Bible Institute, where I had started before being drafted for service in World War II. She wanted to go to college at either Wheaton or Nyack. A girl named Virginia Lacy started attending one of the churches Norma Jean's father started. She had attended Fort Wayne for one year and was very enthused about it. Virginia convinced Norma Jean to look into it. She did, and since it was closer to her family and less expensive than the other schools, she decided to attend. That was where we met.

When we entered the ministry we soon realized that we both had abilities that did not quite fit the traditional roles of men and women. The first thing was keeping the checkbook and handling money. I messed it up, but she did a super job taking care of the finances. She did not like keeping the floors clean, but it was no problem for me. Norma Jean had worked with her father starting churches, so her ideas were far better than mine. All through our fifty-three years of church planting, living together, raising a family, and anything else that needed to be done, we were both able to jump right in and get the job done.

Many times during our marriage, her pharmacist uncle urged her to become a pharmacist. Instead, she chose to use her time and energy to care for the home and children and help with ministry. My dear wife did more than could possibly be expected because she had great ability and drive, and she felt she was doing it for her Lord and Savior, Jesus Christ. She was an excellent housekeeper. The children were always well dressed and cared for. My clothes were clean and pressed, with the shirts ironed better than the professionals. She taught Sunday school classes for over sixty-five years. She planned the services and cut the stencils for the bulletin. She led the Children's Church programs, conducted Vacation Bible School, and planned and directed Christmas programs. A monthly Women's Missionary Society meeting was also one of her responsibilities, and for twenty-five years she led a weekly women's community Bible study. I attribute much of the success we had in ministry together to how God worked through my dear wife, Norma Jean.

BEGINNING IN PLYMOUTH

When Norma Jean and I got back from our honeymoon, we lived in the Bethel College dormitory for about a month, sleeping in bunk beds. But home missions had a church for us in Plymouth, Indiana. The Church Extension Director, Joe Kimble, found a group of people who were interested in opening up a closed church in Plymouth. Since we weren't being accepted on the foreign missions field, he said, "Glenn and Norma Jean, why don't you be home missionaries?" We accepted that call and moved to Plymouth in 1950.

I was leaving $100 a day for $25 a week. I still worked with my brother some, but I turned over the business to him for good. The denomination was furnishing us with an old house, but utilities were not included, and we were paying our own insurance. It had no indoor plumbing, only a hand pump in the kitchen and a dilapidated outhouse. I had grown up in these conditions, and though Norma Jean was a city girl, she was wide open for it.

The house was absolutely filthy when we got there, but the owners said they would buy wallpaper, paint, and other materials if we wanted them. We completely renovated this six-bedroom house, papering, painting, and fixing it up real nice. We

This was our first house together, in Plymouth, IN.

had enough money left after buying a new car to buy a stove, refrigerator, washing machine, table, and a spring mattress. We also had the outhouse fixed up. Norma Jean's Aunt Betty came to visit, and after seeing the outhouse she declared, "Norma Jean, that's the fanciest outhouse I've ever seen!"

Ironically, the man who lived there before us was also named Glenn Marks! In fact, at one time a bill collector came and wanted to collect a bill for Glenn Marks. I wasn't at home at the time, so he said to Norma Jean, "I'm not wanting Glenn Marks the preacher, I want Glenn Marks the builder." Well, I had been a builder too, so the guy still thought we were trying to get out of paying. Finally, Norma Jean told him to go check with the landlord. He came back and told her he was sorry.

The church building in Plymouth was roughly a hundred years old. Jacoby Church had been quite a thriving church at one point. There were a couple of the Jacobys living close by, and they were interested in seeing if it could thrive again. They were the trustees, and it was clear that no work would be done on the church building without their approval. Even so, we repainted the building, got it all cleaned up, and started Sunday evening services. Soon we started Sunday school and Sunday morning services.

It went very well. People were coming, and we got up to fifty or sixty people. Norma Jean was a tremendous help in ministry. Her father had started churches, so she really knew more than I did. She worked with the children and spiritually mentored some young girls she was teaching to play the piano. She also played the piano for the services and helped me plan them.

Most of the people we ministered to in Plymouth were already church people, but there was a lot of spiritual growth. There were also conversions among some young people, especially the three girls

Norma Jean and I inside our first house two months after our wedding.

that Norma Jean mentored.

One Sunday night there was only one older lady in the service, and we'd picked her up. I thought I had a very good sermon prepared, and sermons were coming hard. Boy, I hesitated! I didn't want to use it on just one person! But the Lord said, "No, you've got a sermon, you've got a congregation, so go ahead." So I preached the sermon directly to her. It was on the Twenty-Third Psalm. At the close of the service I went back to shake hands, like I always do, and she told me, "Oh Reverend, you don't know how much I appreciated that sermon. It isn't often that a person gets to hear their funeral sermon before they die." I said, "That sounds real interesting, Grandma Heidi. Tell me about it." She said, "Well, I've left in my papers that I want the minister to preach on the Twenty-Third Psalm for my funeral service, and I feel like I've heard my funeral sermon today."

Two or three years later, after we had left this church, I heard she was ill, and it was convenient to stop in and see her. The first thing she said when I got in the room was, "Reverend, I thought you were going to have to preach that sermon." "Oh no, Grandma Heidi, you're so strong," I replied. "No, I'm gonna be going pretty soon," she said. A couple of months later she died, and the family asked me to come preach the funeral sermon. I used that message, and it was a real challenge to everybody.

It was early in our marriage and ministry, so I was bound to make a few mistakes. One time I walked into the kitchen while my good wife was in the process of making a pie. I saw what she was doing and remarked, "My mother did it another way." I was sincere—I thought the way Mom did it was easier. Norma Jean was making it the way her grandmother taught her, and she didn't appreciate my advice. She took that pie press and threw it in my face! I didn't get a pie for a long time. I certainly learned real quick that's not the thing to say!

I didn't attend seminary, but I began to learn that I could depend on the Holy Sprit to help me in my need, and that built confidence. I was a loner and a timid person as a child, but I had gotten to the place where I had quite a bit of self-confidence. I don't think I ever thought I was a big shot, but I had a relationship with Jesus Christ, and He had given me a message.

We were at the Plymouth church for two years. At that point there was another pastor available, and Reverend Kimble wanted us to take on a new project. About the time we were moving to a different place, the devil really beat us up. We were expecting a baby. It was the normal time, a couple years after we were married, and everything was progressing normally. All the checkups were good, but our baby daughter, Dorothy Mae, was stillborn as a result of malpractice. This was a shocking, devastating experience. Norma Jean grieved deeply. I was strongly tempted to leave the ministry. But Norma Jean's grandmother had gone through a similar experience and was able to help and encourage us. By God's help, we weathered that storm, and soon after we moved to South Bend, Indiana.

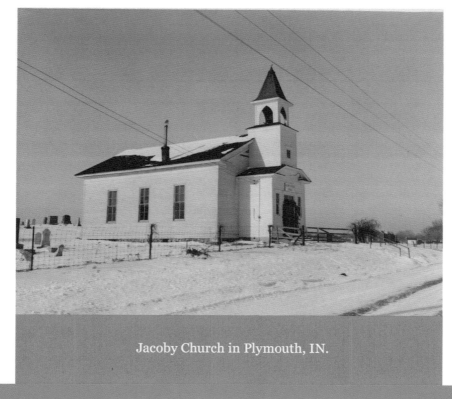

Jacoby Church in Plymouth, IN.

SOME CONVERSIONS IN OUR MINISTRY

At the first church we started in our ministry we were very happy with the new people coming to the services. One family was a young couple and their three children. Hal and Virginia were regular attendees and were willing to help, but we soon became aware that they had never turned their lives over to Jesus and accepted the new birth that He gives. We began to pray for them very earnestly. We had evangelistic meetings for a week, but we were very disappointed that Hal and his family did not attend.

The next Tuesday, Norma Jean received a call from Virginia saying they needed to see us. When we got together, they told us that Hal felt so miserable he had gone to the doctor. We talked and explained that real conviction from the Holy Spirit makes us very miserable. We talked a little more, and then Hal asked if we could pray. Both of them confessed their sins and asked Jesus to forgive them and give them His new birth and life. When they got up from their knees, Hal said, "It seems like I'm looking at the world through rose-colored glasses." They went home rejoicing. Later they told us that the next morning, one of them started to light a cigarette. The other asked, "Are we going to do that, now that we're saved?" With Christ's help, both were able to give up smoking, and they live changed lives. Hal became our Sunday school superintendent, and they continued to serve the Lord.

Later, when we were building the parsonage for the fourth church we started, we had two carpenters working on the building. One was a young man in his early twenties. I'll call him Pete. I worked with them quite a bit and shared the Gospel whenever possible. Pete seemed very interested. One morning, when some other ministers were working with us, Pete said, "Preach, I want to pray and accept Jesus." We all knelt and prayed, and soon Pete had the witness that he had been saved. The next morning when Pete came to work he said, "Preach, look what I have in my pocket." It was a New Testament. He said, "Whenever I reach for a cigarette I will feel this, and I will be able to quit smoking." Sure enough, he quit!

Pete continued smoke-free for a couple of years, but then he got a job as manager of a filling station in another city. I walked in to see him one morning, and he was smoking at his desk. We talked for a while, and then he said, "Preach, I suppose you're wondering about this," and he pointed to his cigarette. I agreed, so he said, "I never touched one until I looked at a pack and said to myself, 'I wonder if I would still like those.' I lit one and have been hooked ever since." This seems to be the way it works. Jesus helps people as they trust and believe. If they willingly go back to their ways of sin, then they have a real battle.

"That if you confess with your mouth 'Jesus is Lord,' and believe in your heart that God raised him from the dead, you will be saved. For it is with your heart that you believe and are justified, and it is with your mouth that you confess and are saved."

Romans 10:9-10

A YOKE AND A STAY CHAIN

For many years I have been challenged by the words of Jesus about His easy yoke. I do not remember where or when I heard it, but I clearly recall a message that was preached on this passage from Matthew 11. One of the preacher's thoughts was that the phrase "my yoke is easy" could also be translated as "my yoke is well-fit."

This idea always stayed in my mind. Then one day we were going through a historic home as a family, and a yoke was displayed above the fireplace. It was in beautiful shape, and it caught my attention. As I continued to look at it, I saw that it was different from any I had ever seen. What I saw that day was an ox yoke created by a skilled craftsman. It was made especially for two oxen of different sizes. It was thicker on one end, and the ring where the load was attached was designed to be closer to the bigger ox. The effect was that even though one ox was smaller, the yoke would still remain level. The ring being closer to the larger ox would force that ox to pull more of the load, so the weaker ox could do the job without being pulled back.

I called my family into the room and preached a sermon right there! As I had heard before, Christ's easy yoke can also mean His well-fit yoke. The reason Christ's yoke is easy is because He pulls the greater part of the load. He carries the heavy end,

"Come to me, all you who are weary and burdened, and I will give you rest. Take my yoke upon you and learn from me, for I am gentle and humble in heart, and you will find rest for your souls. For my yoke is easy and my burden is light."

Matthew 11:28-30

and as long as we do all we can do, we make it. 1 Corinthians 10:13 states that "God is faithful; he will not let you be tempted beyond what you can bear." We are able to bear the load when we pull next to Him.

Similarly, my great-grandfather George Dietrich owned a stay chain. Its purpose was to connect to a hook on the farm wagon frame and to the evener of the stronger horse. With this chain in place, both horses could pull all they could pull, but the stronger horse was pulling more than the weaker horse. I used the same principle in my forty-three years of having ponies. I had to train a lot of colts, so I would hitch them to the wagon with their mother. I always fastened the mother pony with a stay rope so she would pull the load until the colt got big enough to pull his part.

Jesus always expects us to do what we can, but He always takes the greater part of the load.

Drawing by E. Ruth Miller.

KEEPING THE LORD'S DAY

> *"Do not be deceived: God cannot be mocked. A man reaps what he sows."*
>
> Galatians 6:7

Keeping the Lord's Day holy by attending the house of worship, resting, and doing as little work as possible was an important teaching of the church, and we practiced it very diligently in our home as I was growing up. We did as much of the Sunday work as we could on Saturday. We had to feed the animals and milk the cows on Sunday, but hay was brought down on Saturday so all we had to do on Sunday was put it in the manger. Grandpa Marks sharpened more than a thousand saws in his lifetime, and no matter how often he was asked to open his shop on Sunday so his customers could pick up their saws, he always refused. Grandpa Holdeman organized his farm and business so that each field produced a money crop for six years, but during the seventh year it was left for pasture.

Our family's commitment to keeping the Lord's Day was very important to my brother and I when we started our business after we returned from the war. The very first week we were asked to work on Sunday, but we refused, saying we would work until dark on Saturday and begin at dawn on Monday. God blessed our business, and remuneration was above what anyone could have imagined.

Norma Jean and I determined to keep the Lord's Day in our home. Sunday is a very busy day for a pastor's family, but to the best of our ability we worked throughout the week to have the sermon and lessons prepared, as well as the shopping and housework done so that Sunday could run as smoothly as possible. Sunday breakfast and dinner were different from weekday meals, and any time left over was for rest and fellowship with family and friends.

I challenge everyone reading this to be very careful how you keep the Lord's Day. Galatians 6:7 tells us, "Do not be deceived; God cannot be mocked. A man reaps what he sows." As we honor God, He will honor us.

BREAKFAST IN FIVE MINUTES

Because Sunday was such a busy day in our home, Norma Jean and I agreed early on that she would dress the children and prepare the Sunday roast while I fixed breakfast. Scrambled eggs with fried ham, cinnamon rolls (store bought), juice, and coffee became my standard menu, and I enjoyed preparing this meal. I learned quickly, however, that getting the family to the table when it was ready was harder than fixing it. I discovered that a five-minute warning usually did the trick. It became a tradition, and sixty-plus years of preparing Sunday breakfast always included a holler up the stairs: "Breakfast in five minutes!"

PLYMOUTH REFLECTION

When we went to Plymouth, our first pastorate, I left $100 a day for $25 a week. At that time, Norma Jean's mother, Mae Byers, said something that really helped me. My mother-in-law's statement was, "The prosperity of the Lord consists not in the abundance of the things we possess, but in the fewness of our wants." This also reminds me of how I wanted to buy a car right after I got out of the army, but instead gave half my money to a girl so she could go to Africa as a missionary. That experience helped me realize that all I have belongs to the Lord. I wanted to do God's will, and the Lord rewarded me. We got the new car when we needed it. At this time, the idea of service really began to well up in my heart. I knew I wanted to be the Lord's servant.

As chaplain of the VFW, I was recently in a Memorial Day parade. I rode in the car with a young man whom I had married probably twenty years earlier. He told me that when I shared my mother-in-law's statement with him in marital counseling, it meant so much to him. It helped him and many others he shared it with as well. I pray that her statement will continue to bless generations of the Lord's servants.

"The prosperity of the Lord consists not in the abundance of the things we possess, but in the fewness of our wants."

Mae Byers

Top: Our first dog, Laddie.
Bottom: Noma Jean with our dog Laddie.

BUILDING IN SOUTH BEND

Rev. Joe Kimble, the Church Extension Director, was trying to start a lot of churches at this time. He knew I had building experience, so he asked me to take over the construction of some new churches. Joe also asked us to get a church in operation in a suburb of South Bend, Indiana. We agreed to do that and prepared to move to South Bend.

There was no parsonage, but there was enough time that we could build our own home. We were able to borrow $8,500 and build a three-bedroom home on a city lot. The church we were starting was close by. Rev. Kimble got the ministerial association of Bethel College invested in this project, so it was a combination of them and the extension department. It was another new start for us.

At the same time, friends of ours were starting a church in La Porte, and they were three months ahead of us. They were going to open at Christmas, and we weren't going to start until Easter, so we helped them with their church during those three months. That was good experience. Then on Easter Sunday, we opened our church. We had a core group of people, really just one family, and a group of college kids from Bethel. We got up to at least fifty in that new church within a few months. Soon we had a full program of Sunday and Wednesday services.

Then another interesting thing happened. I'm sure this was of the Lord. Norma Jean's father was superintendent of a Jewish mission in New York City, and the family farm was in Pennsylvania. We got the idea that maybe we could fix up the family farm so we could bring kids out of New York City and work with them there. There was another pastor available to take over the South Bend church, so we would get it up and running and then turn it over to him. After that we were going to try to work with Norma Jean's father on the farm.

The home missions department agreed to this, even though we were part of the Missionary Church and Norma Jean's father was part of the Christian Missionary Alliance. We kept working and doing what we could do, but the idea just never developed. However, it did free us up, and soon the Lord gave us an opportunity at North Manchester, Indiana.

Left: Norma Jean in front of our house in South Bend.
Right: I'm standing between our car and our house.

Edison Park Church, South Bend, 1952-1953.

SOUTH BEND REFLECTION

"Who, then, are those who fear the Lord? He will instruct them in the ways they should choose."

Psalm 25:12

When we went to South Bend, the idea that we could depend on the Lord to guide us began to fasten itself in my heart more and more. We depended on the Lord to guide because He sees the whole picture. We built a new house and our daughter Jeanette joined our family while we were at South Bend, which was exciting. Very little happened, however, in ministry. I came to South Bend to supervise construction of new church buildings, and that didn't really pan out. We seriously considered going to work with Norma Jean's father, who was superintendent of an old Jewish mission in New York. We had the old family farm that we thought we could make into a retreat for kids from New York. I resigned quite quickly from the South Bend church, thinking we could go set up the retreat, but the Lord had another plan. We were now free to go to North Manchester. We sold our house, packed up, and moved to a little farming community in eastern Indiana.

THANKSGIVING ON THE FARM

Norma Jean and her father on the PA farm.

My wife's family, the Byers family, owned a 110-acre farm in Cambria County, Pennsylvania. This land had come to the family by an original land grant from William Penn. The property lay dormant for a number of years while owned by a great aunt. In the mid-fifties, Norma Jean's father and an uncle bought it and began restoration. There was a fairly nice house in sound condition, a barn, and a couple other small buildings in rather poor condition.

Restoration became a family project. In 1954, I lived next door to a wholesale plumbing store owned by my landlord, and I was able to purchase an electric water pump and water heater at a very low price. The first project on the farm was to pump all the water out of the open well and clean it out. This well consisted of a six-foot diameter hole about ten feet deep, chiseled out of solid rock. We ran a water line to the house, hooked up the pump and heater, and we had hot and cold water to the kitchen sink. Someone was able to purchase a kitchen range that was wood-burning on one end, an oven in the middle, and had electric burners on the other end. The house already had two really nice bedroom suites and a dining room table and chairs. The fireplace was nice, but not efficient, so Grandpa

Byers bought an Ashley wood-burning heating stove. This was a very safe and efficient heating stove, and it heated the house comfortably.

Thanksgiving was approaching, so the decision was made to enjoy it on the old family farm. Those who were able and who desired to make this adventuresome trip included: Grandpa Byers, who had been born there, Norma Jean's father, two of his brothers, one sister, Norma Jean and I, our one-year-old daughter, Jeanette, and Norma Jean's younger brother and sister, Donald and Laura Lee. When we got to the farm, the long lane was too muddy, so we all piled into the back of the dump truck that was part of the farm equipment and drove up the muddy lane to the house. We brought along the turkey and most of the trimmings. We enjoyed a wonderful meal and did a lot of reminiscing about the "good old days." Even though it happened about sixty years ago, the memories of that day still bring me a great amount of pleasure.

MY NORMA JEAN

Norma Jean and I on my eightieth birthday in 2005.

By Glenn Marks
July 10, 1987

I think that I shall never see,
A woman as lovely and good as thee.

With hair so soft and eyes so bright,
And face that expresses your soul's delight.

With voice so gentle and body so sweet,
Being with you is such a treat.

Of character noble, you I can trust.
You satisfy fully—I do not lust.

A mother superb is what you are,
Surpassing all others, really by far.

And grandmother also, you have such a way,
The grandchildren love you in work and in play.

As homemaker, too, you are so great.
Lucky, lucky me, how did I ever rate?

The future is bright with you by my side,
Facing life's challenges, the Lord as our guide.

When time upon earth is finished and done,
Together in heaven we'll be with God's Son.

With worship and praise to God up above
For letting us live this life in our love.

BUILDING AND BEING BUILT UP IN NORTH MANCHESTER

A small group of believers in North Manchester, Indiana, wanted to start a church. They had seen their former church slowly drift away from preaching a Christ-centered Gospel message and were praying that the Lord would send a pastor who had a heart for Christ and His message to their group.

They were acquainted with a pastor in Elkhart whose son attended Bethel College. The son spoke highly of the college and its reputation of biblical teaching and holy living. LaRue Dawes, one of the ladies from the group, wrote and sent a letter about their situation, addressing it simply, "The President – College in Mishawaka." President Goodman of Bethel received the letter and passed it on to Joe Kimble, the Director of Church Extension for the Missionary Church. Joe met with the families and encouraged them to start having prayer meetings. It seemed like an ideal situation for starting a church.

Property became available for building, but Joe, with a heavy heart, had to tell the group that the Conference didn't have the money to buy the

Another photo from the construction of our church in North Manchester.

property. Mrs. Dawes said to him, "Brother Kimble, the Conference may not have the money, but our God has! You just wait. We are going to have our church, all right!" Joe was touched by their faith, but he knew of no way to get the money. He drove home from the meeting, crying nearly all the way. Sure enough, though, the money came in and the property was acquired. The extension department agreed to finance the building project, and construction began in the fall of 1953.

Now a pastor was needed. Our plans to convert the Byers family farm into a camp for kids from New York didn't work out, so God had us ready to move on. We received the call to go to North Manchester in December of 1953.

We drove down from South Bend on a snowy Wednesday afternoon to join the group for a prayer meeting that evening. Our daughter Jeanette was just three weeks old. The people fell in love with her and welcomed us with open arms. This group of sincere believers, mostly hard-working farmers who were hungry for God's Word, won our hearts. We accepted the call to pastor and help with the church building. Within a few weeks we found a

Building the church in North Manchester.

little house a few blocks from Main Street and, with great expectation, began our time of ministry and building in this quiet, rural community.

Construction of the building had been progressing, and before winter set in, the foundation and first floor were completed. Then we had to stop work for about six weeks. This gave us time, however, to concentrate on reaching out to the community. We put a picture in the local paper of our proposed plan and gave the location of our prayer meeting. The Lord used this to bring a family to our group that was not only a vital part of the work in North Manchester, but also became lifelong friends.

The local paper came out on Tuesday. Maxine Deneve walked down the lane of their dairy farm to get the mail and opened the newspaper as she was walking back. The picture caught her attention, she started to read, and before she got back to the house, she knew the Lord was telling her, "This is your church!"

Maxine's family was in a similar situation as the original group. Their church didn't feel they needed Jesus as the Head, the Sacrifice, and the Way to God. The church had strayed from this basic spiritual emphasis. As Sunday School teachers, they had been told to avoid talking about the cross, so as not to scare the kids. This was too much for them, and they were really looking for a new church.

So, Maxine, her husband Al, and their children showed up the next evening for prayer meeting and jumped in feet-first. Maxine was vivacious and energetic. She worked alongside Norma Jean in developing the children's programs. Al was quiet, thoughtful, and deeply spiritual. We were getting ready to start services in the new building on Easter Sunday, and we asked Al if he would be Sunday School superintendent. He said, "I've never done anything like this at all, but if you'll pray for me, I'll do it." And he did it, because he was dependent on the Lord, not himself.

A family photo from 1955, near the beginning of our time at North Manchester.

Our goal was to have Easter service in the new building. In spite of our best efforts, Saturday before Easter came and there was still much to do. An interested couple came by in the morning and commented, "It's very plain to see you are not going to be ready by tomorrow morning!" However, everyone came together, we worked until midnight, and the building was ready for Easter Sunday! We had over a hundred people in attendance.

With the building basically finished, we could now concentrate on growing the congregation and the ministries of the church. We also grew and developed in our roles and abilities as a pastor and wife team. We learned that Norma Jean was a "what-to" person and I was a "how-to" person. She could see what needed to be done, and I was able to come through and make it happen. Norma Jean led the children's programs, planned the services, played piano, and took care of the "secretarial" duties. I led the building projects, studied for sermons and Bible studies, and made home and hospital visits while keeping up with new and established contacts. These roles worked for us and helped us tremendously during all our ministry.

Our family was growing as well. Our daughter Marlene was born in January of 1956, and our son Thomas arrived in May of 1959. Our days were busy and full of caring for our family and church family. But we were doing what we loved and were called to do. It was a very happy time.

Our ministry in North Manchester continued until 1959. Then, though we loved the work and the people, we sensed it was time to turn it over to someone else and move on to a new place where our gifts and abilities could be used more effectively. John Moran, a young, engaging pastor who would later become president of the denomination, took over, and we looked forward to our the next step in building God's Kingdom.

NORTH MANCHESTER REFLECTION

> *"...a good and spacious land, a land flowing with milk and honey..."*
>
> Exodus 3:8

That is how we would describe North Manchester. The people were warm and caring, inviting us regularly into their homes for meals and fellowship. The members of the original group were lifelong friends, supporting us with prayer and encouragement even after we left.

Our ministry built up others and, we believe, had an enduring impact. In the late 70s the church asked us to come back. We gave considerable thought to returning, but in the end remained in Lowell. The church has continued to thrive and share the message of Christ in the community.

BUILDING AND BELIEVING IN INDIANAPOLIS

The Missionary Church had its roots in the spiritual revivals of the late nineteenth century. By the 1950s there were congregations scattered across Ohio, Indiana, Michigan, Pennsylvania, and a few of the western states. Most of these were in small towns and rural communities. The denomination had long wanted to plant a church in Indianapolis, the fast-growing capital of Indiana, but it had not happened. I attended a minister's conference in 1959, where the idea of an Indianapolis church plant was revisited. In spite of the difficulties and uncertainties of such a venture, I knew the Lord was asking me to be willing to move my family to Indianapolis and give ourselves whole-heartedly to planting a church in this urban mission field. Norma Jean agreed, the church extension committee promised help and support, and within a few months things were in motion for the move and the church plant.

Challenges and obstacles came almost immediately. We had only one family in Indianapolis that was strongly committed to the church plant, and it soon became evident that they were not convinced I was the man for the job. Joe Kimble, who was still Church Extension Director, found land for a future building. However, on the evening before closing, the owners called and backed out of the sale. Under these circumstances, we began to seriously reconsider.

After much prayer and seeking direction from the Lord and others, we decided to step out in faith, move to the community, and believe that God would help us share the Gospel in Indianapolis. We found a house available to rent for three months, the home missions department and others with a heart for the area promised financial support, and we trusted that by the end of those three months we would know if we should stay or move on.

Those three months were spent canvassing neighborhoods and trying to develop relationships with neighbors and within the community. I also started a Boys Club, and through that came in contact with many families. By the end of the three months we needed a new house and a place to begin holding services.

We found another rental house close by. On moving day a curious neighbor boy hung around to watch. I talked with him a little and invited him to the Boys Club. In the course of the conversation, he mentioned that his church was moving into its new building soon. "Where are you meeting now?" I asked. "In the Community Center," he answered. I checked that out, and within a few weeks the other church moved out and we could begin holding Sunday morning services there.

From that point, things began to take off. The original family, though still not sure I was the right man for the job, was very involved and worked alongside us. More families started to come. It soon became evident that we needed a permanent location. But land at a reasonable price was seemingly non-existent. Everything, especially in the northeastern part of town, was booming, and the vast acres of farmland were already sold to house and business developers. We needed to truly believe God for land to build His church.

The answer came through a young couple attending our services. They told me about eight-and-a-half acres of land an uncle tried to buy, but for which the sale did not go through. We immediately went to investigate.

The property definitely had its drawbacks. It was landlocked, and the ramshackle house and garage would need to be destroyed. However, trying to look at it through "God's eyes," we could see definite

Our house in Indianapolis, complete with the garage chapel.

possibilities. The area was growing daily. Four houses a day were being built on one side of the property, and just as many on the other side! Here was enough land for a church and a parsonage, right in the middle of all this growth.

We began negotiations with the owners. The deal that fell through was five acres for $35,000. We were able to buy all eight-and-a-half acres of this property for $10,000! An additional $800, acquired by the sale of a small adjacent lane, brought the road through, connecting the property to a main road on one end and the housing development on the other end. What a miracle!

The next step was, of course, seeking God's direction in how to use this property to build His church and further His kingdom. We knew we weren't ready for a church building, but we needed our own meeting place. Again the answer came to us through a neighbor. We couldn't afford the daily paper, but a kind neighbor often brought hers over after she had read it. A house plan was featured in one of those papers, and it caught our attention. It was a four-bedroom Cape Cod with a full basement and attached garage. The more we looked at the plans, the more we could envision the house being perfect for our family during the week and perfect for our growing congregation on Sundays. With only slight adjustments, we could use the full basement for the children's classrooms and activities, the main living area for adult classes, and the garage as a small chapel. We presented this idea to the district leaders and the community. Amazingly, it was approved, and I began building this house for my family and

Norma Jean and I in the sanctuary of Providence Missionary Church in Indianapolis.

the family of God.

Changes to the garage and the family room, though relatively minor, made the difference in being able to use the house as a temporary church. Rather than putting on garage doors, I put in double doors. The garage backed right up to the family room, which was a few steps higher. Instead of a normal wall between the garage and family room, I put in two six-foot doors with concealed hinges. When completed, it served its purpose even better than we could have imagined. During the week, our family could live comfortably and enjoy a spacious family room. But on Saturday night I'd take out four screws in the baseboard, four screws on a board by the ceiling, and open up the doors. A pulpit was placed in the middle of the family room, and it was now a platform for the garage chapel. As a family, we did not use the garage or the basement, so they remained set up throughout the week. The living room and dinette were also available for Sunday School classes.

As much as we loved our new home and were pleased with the possibilities it provided, our calling and work was to share the Gospel of Christ. By now it was the early 1960s, and the world was changing a lot. The television was just becoming popular. The Vietnam War was going on, John F. Kennedy and Martin Luther King, Jr. were assassinated, and the Civil Rights Movement was in full swing. I knew what was happening, but I didn't worry much about it. I preached and lived Christ as best I knew. The big city was very different from what I was used to, but I didn't adapt my ministry much. I just said, "Lord, I don't have a 'thing.' If I'm going to minister to these people, the Holy Spirit is going to have to come tell me what to say, what to preach, how to contact them, and how to enter into their problems." And He did. The only real change we made was emphasizing the children's ministry even more—this was the Baby Boom, after all. We were able to start with the children and then reach their families.

I did a tremendous amount of calling on people, door-to-door. New families were moving almost daily into the developments around us, and I wanted to simply introduce myself and let them know about the church we were starting. It was always well-received, and some would even want to talk about spiritual things during the call.

One such call challenged me more than most. I called on the family of a boy in our Boys Club. His mother looked me in the eye and said. "Reverend, one church says to believe this and another church says to believe something else. How in the world is a person supposed to know what is right?" I gave her all the answers that I had and then went back to my study feeling confused and defeated. I said to God, "I need to have more answers. I can't continue the ministry with these people unless you give me the answer to that question: How do we know what to believe?"

The Lord gave me two verses. The first was Matthew 5:6, "Blessed are those who hunger and

This photo appeared in an issue of the Indianapolis News and the front cover of *The Gospel Banner* in 1962. The sleigh belonged to my great-grandparents and was almost a hundred years old at the time. We were part of an entry that won our church second place in the local Christmas parade.

thirst for righteousness, for they will be filled." The second verse was John 7:17. Jesus was being accused of just being a man, and He answered, "Anyone who chooses to do the will of God will find out whether my teaching comes from God or whether I speak on my own." So, if I am hungry for righteousness and choose to do the will of God, the Holy Spirit will guide me into what is right. I was able to answer her question, and later she knelt in our living room and accepted Jesus. These verses have helped me and many others throughout my ministry.

Another call brought us in contact with a lovely family. The wife Connie and the children started coming to services. She had some spiritual background but now found a renewed faith and joy in the Lord. Her husband Bob was head of security for a large chain of department stores, and he was more reserved about spiritual things. He was very nice and respectful, but also skeptical about church and Christ.

Plans to vacation at a dude ranch had to be cancelled when they found out they were expecting their fourth child. So Norma Jean said, "Hey, come to camp meeting with us!" We found a place for them

Providence Missionary Church, Indianapolis, IN.

to stay, and the whole family came to Prairie Camp. Afterwards I called on Bob, and he said, "Reverend, when I saw that many good people together in one place, I knew there had to be something genuine." Bob accepted Christ as his Savior and became a very active member in our church.

We continued with services in the garage chapel for a few years. We averaged 197 with a high of 210. By 1964 we knew we had the means and stability to build. We chose the spot on the property, got the plans approved, and found a retired minister with a lot of building experience to supervise construction. Everything was set to go. However, one week before construction was to begin, the retired minister had a heart attack. The doctor told him he could do nothing but the essentials.

What were we going to do? Should we hold up the building project, or should I take over and run it? I was really scared! I had been involved with building supervision, but nothing this big. And how could I pastor as well? But as I was kneeling beside my bed and praying, "Lord give me wisdom," I received assurance: "Go ahead, I'll help you." I had recently read in Exodus 35:30-35 that God gave Bezalel and Oholiab wisdom in how to build the tabernacle in the wilderness, and also how to teach. I was able to believe the Lord that I could handle supervising the building project and continue as pastor. Thankfully, there were no major difficulties, everyone helped as they could, and the building was completed on schedule. We moved into the new building in the fall of 1964.

In the midst of all this busyness, our children were still our first responsibility. Cynthia Sue joined our family in June of 1960, so now we had four young children. We have always been deeply thankful for God's provision for our family. In spite of being on district support of only $47 a week, we never felt poor. We had a lovely home, a big yard for the kids to play in, a huge garden to provide fresh food, and a strong church community for fellowship and support. There were very few extras, but Norma Jean somehow made the money stretch for food and clothes. A good education was extremely important to her, and she helped Jeanette and Marlene get a good start in school.

So, things were beginning to settle down, and life was good. We were enjoying our family and our ministry. We could see ourselves staying here a long time. Little did we know what was waiting for us around the corner.

The original family, in spite of their misgivings, remained with us and was very active in the church. Even though we now had a building and the church had grown from almost nothing to a congregation of over two hundred, the husband still didn't believe I was the right man and could keep the church growing. In the spring of 1966, he called the church board together and convinced them to ask for our resignation.

Under the circumstances, we felt we had to leave, and leave quickly. We had no place to go and no prospects. Now more than ever we needed to trust our Heavenly Father and believe that He would show us the next step.

INDIANAPOLIS REFLECTION

"Jesus said, 'Everything is possible for him who believes.' Immediately the boy's father exclaimed, "I do believe; help me overcome my unbelief!"'

Mark 9:23-24

Looking back, we see Indianapolis as a time of proving and refining our faith. From the beginning to the end we had to stand on the promises of God and believe that "Jesus Christ is the same yesterday, today and forever" (Hebrews 13:8). In spite of the uncertainties, the obstacles, our own weaknesses, and the changing times, people came to know Christ, and lives were changed.

Being asked to resign was a shock and brought a very difficult year for our family. However, in the end we were able to forgive and trust that "in all things God works for the good of those who love him, who have been called according to his purpose" (Romans 8:28). We could accept that our work there was done and it was time for us to leave.

In contrast to North Manchester, the church continued only a few years after we left. The building, however, has continued to be used by various congregations.

Top: Worship service in the garage chapel.
Bottom: Children's church in the basement.

ROLLAN J. GONGWER: A LETTER

Dear Pastor Marks,

I don't know if you will remember me or not, but God has laid it on my heart to write to you. If you're like me, you sometimes wonder what your influence has been on other people.

In the 1960s I was attending pre-med courses in Bloomington, IN, at IU, and we were planning on coming to Indianapolis for medical school. (That didn't work out; I became an optometrist instead; Jeremiah 29:11). But when we were planning that way, we visited the Missionary Church you were pastoring in Indianapolis on Sunday morning. I don't remember what you said, but it was on tithing, and it changed our way of giving. Now, over forty years later, and with many years of tithing and giving above the tithe to God's work, it is time to give you credit for the way God has prospered us in obedience to His Word through you, His messenger, many yeas ago.

I spent sixteen years in a private practice in Cassopolis, MI, and then was led to join the Commissioned Corps of the US Public Health Service and serve in the Indian Health Service (IHS). I served in the IHS for twenty years—in Montana (five), Arizona (three), and Oklahoma (12)—before retiring in Oro Valley, AZ, in 2004. During that time we worshipped in different churches from thirty-five to 300 people. Now God has blessed greatly in giving us a place of service in the Oro Valley Church of the Nazarene. When we came to Oro Valley three years ago, they had just broken ground for the new sanctuary. In the last two years we have grown from about 500 by one hundred each year to an average of 700 today. God has blessed us so that Carol and I are able to help support three missionaries, three children overseas, and various Christian organizations that are doing humanitarian work as well as spreading the Gospel, and that in addition to supporting our local church. You had a part in all of this because God used you to teach us to tithe (Malachi 3:10), even while borrowing a lot of money for college many years ago, and because God has been faithful to us.

Thank you for your faithfulness to God in Indianapolis on one special Sunday morning in the 1960s! I just wanted you to know how your words impacted one couple out of the many you ministered to over your lifetime, and how that has been a part of God's work in many parts of the country over the years!

God's blessings on you and your family,

Rollan J. Gongwer, O.D., F.A.A.O.

USPHS, Capt., Retired

June 24, 2007

BRIDGING TO A BETTER PLACE

Being asked to resign from the church in Indianapolis left us stunned and wondering what we should do. It wasn't long, however, before two different churches were in contact with us and wanted us to come and pastor. One was an established church with another denomination in Pontiac, MI. The other was a new church plant with our own denomination in Ohio. Both of the opportunities came at the same time, and there were good reasons to prayerfully consider both. The day came when we had to make a choice, and we had not been able to decide.

I got up early that morning, found a secluded spot to park the car, and began believing God for the right answer. I prayed, "Lord, what in the world should I do? How do I know what Your will is?" I looked out the windshield of my car, and there in the clouds was a clear image of the state of Michigan! I had no doubt this was God's answer. I found a pay phone, called the church in Pontiac, and told them that we would accept the offer to be their pastor. So, in the summer of 1966, we prepared to move to Pontiac, MI, a town just thirty miles northwest of Detroit.

Things did not start out well. A heavy platter fell and broke the nose of a dear friend who came to help us move. Tom, Cindy, and I became very ill from food poisoning a few days before moving. We pushed through that, though, and arrived in Pontiac on schedule. The moving van did not arrive that same day, so we needed to get a motel for the night. We took the first and cheapest room we could find, but discovered that we were sharing the room with several cockroaches. The night was spent with the lights on and a rolled-up newspaper close by. The next morning we could hardly wait to get out of there and drive to our new house.

The Pontiac church owned some property and was planning to sell the building they were in and build a new one. That was one of the main reasons they wanted me to be their pastor. There was a house on that land. When we agreed to come, we asked if we could move

into that house. It was old, but the property had trees, a large pond, and lots of open space. When we arrived, however, they asked us to move into the parsonage by the existing church instead. The parsonage was newer and nicer in some respects, but the location of the house was very undesirable. The church was five feet away on one side, and an old house was ten feet away in the back. The house on the other side was fifteen feet away, and there was not one tree in the yard. To top it off, every time we looked out our front window, we saw a condemned house across the street. This was not what we had expected, but surely things would get better.

The children settled into school, and we began to acquaint ourselves with the people and ministry. The congregation welcomed us, we found the children's programs and women's ministry to be vibrant and active, and since the building project had not begun, I enjoyed concentrating on preaching and calling on the families in Pontiac.

It wasn't long, though, before we began to sense some underlying problems. No matter what we tried or suggested, the church did not experience growth, and the people seemed content with that. We discovered the church had come from a split. They were very critical of the former congregation and anyone who did not "measure up" to a certain level of spirituality. I remember talking with one of the men in leadership who was speaking negatively about a neighbor. "Have you ever invited him to church or shared the Gospel?" I asked. He had not thought of that.

A year went by, and I began to question if we were in the right place. It did not appear that the church was going to begin building. Though my family was adjusting, they were not happy. I wondered if my ministry was effective. I shared these concerns with the District Superintendent, but he asked us to stay on another year. We reluctantly agreed.

On a much larger scale, the country was experiencing great unrest. Racial tensions were growing, and riots were breaking out in major cities across the country. On July 23, 1967, a police raid on an unlicensed bar in downtown Detroit sparked one of the worst riots in our history. The Michigan National Guard and the 82nd Airborne Division, as well as state and local police, were called in. After five days, there were forty-three people dead, 1,189 injuries, over 7,000 arrests, and 2,000 buildings destroyed. It was chaotic, and all this was happening so close.

At first we thought it would be confined to Detroit, but it wasn't. On Wednesday after the Detroit riots started, I went fishing with a man whose wife attended our church. I was hoping to have a chance to talk about spiritual things with him. He caught several fish, but for my part, neither the fishing nor the sharing was successful. Coming back that afternoon, we found out that rioting had started in downtown Pontiac, just a few miles from our home, and the National Guard had been called in to bring the situation under control. All of this was brought very close to home that night when vandals set fire to the condemned building across the street.

Things were quite a mess. We responded by praying that God would intervene and bring reconciliation. We also prayed for protection. Our children were aware of the situation, but seemed secure in our confidence that God was in control.

Within a few weeks after these events, our time in Pontiac was brought to an end. It had nothing to do with the riots or the ministry; it was church politics. A pastor had to leave a church in Grand Rapids. He had much more seniority than I did, and the District Superintendent asked me to resign so the other pastor could come to Pontiac. On one hand, we were relieved to be leaving, but on the other, we could not believe this was happening again. We were out of a job and had nowhere to go.

Norma Jean and I turned to our Almighty God. Fear and bitterness began to creep in, but He kept us at peace. In an odd turn of events, which we came to see as providential, Norma Jean's father was asked

to take the church vacated by the pastor coming to Pontiac. The parsonage there was very large. By the middle of August, our family of six and our dog, Holly, left for Grand Rapids, and we moved in with Norma Jean's parents. We knew it could only be temporary, but we had a place to live. We would wait on the Lord for direction and the next step.

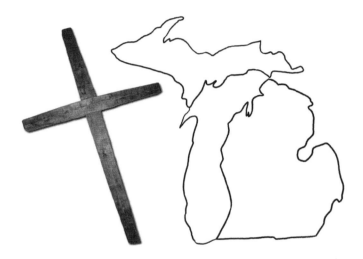

HOW SATAN TRIED TO DISCOURAGE AND DESTROY

"Resist the devil, and he will flee from you."

James 4:7

Throughout my entire lifetime Satan has tried continually to keep me from serving Jesus in an effectual way. Sometimes he has tried to take my life. But God has sent His angels to protect from these moral, emotional, spiritual, and physical attacks in order to keep me here to serve Him. I have had the confidence that if I hang in there, the devil will flee from me. I have been determined to go ahead, to not let Satan beat me out of the things I felt Jesus wanted me to do.

It seems that his attacks come in fives:

I. Spiritual attacks:

1. As a child and teenager I had an up-and-down relationship with Jesus. Sometimes things went really well, and other times I felt like the good little bad boy. However, the Lord preserved me in the faith.

2. At one time, Satan convinced me that I had committed the unpardonable sin. A Bible school student helped me see that it was just Satan's lie.

3. Early in my ministry I thought I was too short to be effective as a minister. The taller men had the large churches and the positions of leadership. I was reminded of my father's statement, "You can't tell by the size of the frog how far he will jump," and this helped me immensely.

4. At one point I began to think I needed some special spiritual experience like the ones I read about other leaders having. Even with much seeking, I never got one. In time, I understood that Jesus wanted to give me a "Glenn Marks experience," not anyone else's experience.

5. I went through quite a period of depression because nothing seemed to be working out right. At Prairie Camp the evangelist said to me, after all other advice had failed, "Brother Marks, you have four teenagers who are serving the Lord—you must have done something right." This was a great help to me.

II. Health:

1. I had asthma, both as a child and later in life.

2. I got tuberculosis and whooping cough in Indianapolis, but they were detected early and I received good treatment.

3. Later in life I found out I had prostate cancer. I underwent radical treatment and have been cancer-free for more than ten years!

4. The Lord helped me through a knee replacement, poor circulation, and ankle problems.

5. I have had an irregular heartbeat for more than eight years, but I'm still alive!

III. Circumstances:

1. When I was earning $100 a day while at Bethel College, I was tempted to stay in business rather than going into ministry as planned. Thankfully, God used Norma Jean to set me straight.

2. When we lost our first baby, we asked ourselves, "Is this the kind of God we're serving?"

3. I was asked to resign at our third church plant.

4. While I was building churches I earned $800 that I never got, and I thought I needed. Eventually I decided I could live without it better than the man who cheated me could live with it.

5. When I retired, the conference requested that a pastor not attend the church from which he had retired. We owned our home and wanted to stay. Thankfully, we were able to make arrangements with the church and new pastor.

IV. Satan tried to take my life in the army:

1. Because I did not kneel and pray before getting into my bunk my first night in the army, confessing Jesus before men, God the Father and the angels could not help me (Matthew 10:32, Luke 12:8). My personal life was not what it should have been, and I was not able to witness. If I had not had a father that the Holy Spirit could burden to pray for my safety the two nights we were fighting to capture the dam on the Rur River, I am totally convinced I would have been killed.

2. An enemy shell was shot at our vehicle, but we were spared.

3. This happened two more times, and still the Lord kept me from harm.

4. One time a shell landed between two of us. The other man's leg was injured, but I was preserved.

5. There was a direct hit of a shell that destroyed the house we had slept in the night before. It probably hit within an hour of us leaving.

V. Satan tried to to take my life as a civilian:

1. The first time was when I was eight or nine years old. My daddy had started to build a garage, and I'm sure that he ran out of money before he could finish, so he had just the outside walls and the cross tier completed. My brother and I thought it was just great playing up there, and Dad let us do it. A carpenter needed to be able to balance and not be afraid. One day I was having a fun time on this frame, and all was well until one of the boards moved as I stepped on it. I fell nine feet to the concrete floor and landed on my head. The next thing I knew I was lying in my grandfather's bed with ice on my head and the doctor at my side. It had been just a few hours! The good Lord had protected me, and I survived this incident with no permanent injury.

2. Another time my brother and I had been putting a wood shingle roof on a barn. We had finished the shingles and taken down the scaffold. The only thing we hadn't finished was the metal ridgepole that completed the top. We had to wait for this, so we took the scaffold down to use on another job. When we went back to put on the ridgepole, I was at the top of the roof. Suddenly, I started to slip down the roof. I couldn't stop myself until I got right at the edge, ready to fall all the way to the ground. My brother told me to just rest quiet. He got down, got a ladder, and saved me. If I had slipped that far, there was no reason I shouldn't have kept slipping—except that the Lord stopped and miraculously held me there. I certainly would have been injured if I had fallen sixteen feet to the ground.

3. Another time that the Lord was merciful and protected me was when I was starting a job remodeling a church in Battle Creek. I was there alone, working in the attic above the sanctuary. I was sure that the electric was shut off on a particular line. I went to cut off the wire and my hand froze. There was still power in it. I couldn't move. There was nobody else there, and I couldn't open my hand. What was I going to do? I got the idea that I might be able to fall off and pull my hand away. That's a dangerous thing to do because I could have gone through the ceiling. I fell off, hit a joist, and pulled my hand away. Otherwise, I know I would have been killed.

4. I was helping put on the roof decking in a church in Flint, which was one of my specialties. We were on a scaffold about twenty feet up when I lost my

balance and started to fall off the side. However, I was able to reach out and touch the ceiling. If I had been alone I'd have been in a tragic situation, but someone was able to come up and pull me back, so I didn't fall. I'd have been killed sure as the world!

5. Finally, I was on my way back home after helping a builder. Norma Jean was having some problems and I wasn't getting good sleep. It was evening and I knew I was getting sleepy, so I had decided to stop and rest after the next turn. Before I got there I went out like a light. I crossed the center line and sideswiped a car. There was no human injury, but my car was totaled after I swerved back and hit the berm. I had just dropped my collision insurance, but a used car put me back in business and building churches.

> *"For he will command his angels concerning you to guard you in all your ways."*
>
> Psalm 91:11

ANOTHER PROFITABLE CALL

All through my ministry I did a lot of house-to-house visitations to get acquainted with people, to see if I could help them spiritually, and to see if I could minister to them in my churches. While we were at our fifth church plant I made a call on a man and found that we had some things in common: we had both been in World War II.

I shared with him how my life had been spared because we got out of a house we had slept in just about an hour before a direct hit from a shell demolished it. He shared that he was in North Africa and part of the invasion at Anzio. He was in a foxhole and had a tremendous urge to get out. It seemed like a very dumb thing to do because it was during an air raid. As soon as he got out of the foxhole, another man jumped in. That man was killed while my friend went all through the war without ever being wounded.

As I got better acquainted with this man (I'll call him Joe), he began to open his heart and share his past life with me. Joe had heard me talk about camp meeting, and he told me about his camp meeting experiences. As a teenager, Joe had gone to camp meeting and really found the Lord Jesus as his Savior. He became quite enthusiastic about his new life, and he met a young lady who he continued to date. They matured and began to talk about marriage and their life work. The young lady was certain that God wanted her to be a foreign missionary. Joe became hesitant. He loved her very much and wanted to marry her, but he thought she was too frail to be a missionary. Joe became so adamant in this belief that the lady broke off their relationship. She married another man, they became foreign missionaries, she had several children, and things went very well for her.

Poor Joe, he was devastated. He joined the army and spent his life trying to prove to himself that there really couldn't be anything to this religion business. When I met him he was an unhappy, broken man. He had married and had a couple of children, but his wife was gone. He was living with his son, but their relationship was not good.

The good news about this story is that as our relationship grew, Joe admitted his wrong, confessed his sin, and again turned his heart and life over to Jesus. He died knowing that things were right with Jesus and he was going to heaven.

> *"If we confess our sins, he is faithful and just and will forgive us our sins and purify us from all unrighteousness."*
>
> 1 John 1:9

PONTIAC REFLECTION

> *"Though the fig tree does not bud and there are no grapes on the vines, though the olive crop fails and the fields produce no food, though there are no sheep in the pen and no cattle in the stalls, yet I will rejoice in the Lord, I will be joyful in God my Savior."*
>
> Habakkuk 3:17-18

We saw very little fruit for our labor in the short time we were in Pontiac. The way things ended left us questioning whether we should have even gone there. "Should we have gone to Ohio?" was an easy question to ask. I was confident, though, that God heard my desperate plea when we did not know where to go and led us to Pontiac. In time we could see clearly that it was just a stepping stone, a bridge to bring us to Lowell, where our family and ministry could thrive.

Things worked out wonderfully for the church in Ohio, and that has been further confirmation that the decision was right. A young man from the denomination felt the call to preach. He was very successful pastoring the church in Ohio we considered taking. He went on to pastor one of the largest churches in the denomination. Then he became a District Superintendent, and after that the President of the denomination. The Lord used us going to Michigan to make all that happen.

BUILDING AND A BREATH OF FRESH AIR AT MEADOWVIEW

Norma Jean's father was an early riser, often taking a walk before breakfast. He would buy the morning paper on his way home, and while the rest of us were just getting the day started, he had already thoroughly read the newspaper. This habit provided us with our next home. One morning, after only a few weeks with them, he noticed a short, simple ad: "For rent, house in the country. Write if interested." Only a P.O. box was given. So, with no more information and only a sense that we should try, Norma Jean wrote a letter describing our family and circumstances. We received a response shortly saying that our letter had been chosen and providing information on how we could see the house.

Norma Jean, the children, and I piled into our rusty Pontiac station wagon and drove east from Grand Rapids out into the beautiful countryside around Lowell. Arriving at the house, we could hardly believe our eyes. The "house in the country" was a large, white farmhouse on a two-hundred-acre dairy farm. The old but charming farmhouse with its oak floors and woodwork, the garden plot just beside it, and the huge barns and acres of farmland all stirred a sense of hope and healing within us. Even the name, Meadowview Farm, made us happy. Our hearts said, "We'll take it!" But our wallets said, "Impossible!" I was still unemployed and had no firm job prospects.

The owner, a retired head of surgical services at Butterworth Hospital, had invited us to come by his house afterwards to give him our decision. We drove the short distance to their home, a large, inviting log cabin in the woods, and told him and his wife our situation. By the grace of God, they did not send us on our way. They took time to talk with Norma Jean, the children (who were, thankfully, on their best behavior), and me. They wanted to make it

work for us. When they found out my background in building and construction, the Doctor said, "I have a lot of work I need done on the farm and my place. I'm sure we can work something out!" We came to an agreement and drove away, praising and thanking God.

Things went remarkably well. We moved into the farmhouse in time for the kids to start school. The Doctor gave me plenty of work and paid immediately in cash. There was always enough for rent and groceries.

The fix-it jobs I did for the Doctor did not pay for all the expenses that our family of six had, of course. I knew I needed to do something more. While still in Pontiac, I helped a pastor from Marshall, MI, get the plans he needed for his new church building from a company in Grand Rapids. The Lord gave me the idea to see if I could help this pastor build a church for less than planned, and also make enough income to pay our bills. Being forced to supervise the Indianapolis building project, and seeing how well it went and the money we saved, gave me courage to

Our ponies Queenie and Princess pulling a sleigh at Meadowview. In the sleigh are Norma Jean's sister Laura Lee, her husband Ben, and baby Pammy. Our dog Holly is behind the sleigh.

stick my neck out and try.

The whole idea fit together with amazing speed. I helped the pastor and congregation build the new church they needed, and I could now adequately support my family. In fact, the idea worked so well that the building company lined up other congregations I could help supervise.

We lived at Meadowview for four years, from 1967 to 1971. The children were happy in the schools and excelled in their schoolwork. It was here that God finally granted my desire to get a pony for my kids. The Doctor let us ride all over the farmland and use the barns freely. In so many ways, the time we spent at Meadowview was just what my family needed.

Our son Tom on Buffy at Meadowview Farm.

Our daughter Cindy on Buffy at Meadowview Farm.

MEADOWVIEW MEMORIES

Our years at Meadowview were mostly quiet and uneventful. There are three incidents, however, that could have ended very badly. We have always been very thankful for God's mercy and protection. This is a short account of those three incidents.

. . .

A Halloween Scare

While building churches, I traveled a lot and occasionally had to be gone overnight. One evening, close to Halloween, I was out of town, so Norma Jean and the children were alone at home. Sometime after dark there was a knock on the door. When Norma Jean answered, two men she didn't recognize were there. The men said they were having car trouble and asked if they could come in and use the phone. Norma Jean said, "If you give me the number, I will call. You can just wait here on the porch." The men became insistent that they come into the house, and they also began making other odd demands. Norma Jean was trying to remain calm, but she was getting very frightened. Suddenly our gentle collie dog, Holly, came to the front porch and gave a threatening growl. "Does your dog bite?" the men asked. "Not unless I tell her to!" replied Norma Jean. The men quickly got into their car "that was having trouble" and drove away.

. . .

Roger and the Clothesline

Meadowview Farm had once been home to about forty prize Jersey cows. These were sold before we moved in, but a tenant farmer was still farming the land. A crop dusting plane would spray the fields periodically, swooping back and forth very close to the house. We never knew when the plane was coming.

A neighbor girl, Suzanne, owned a very large quarter horse named Roger. He was at least sixteen hands high. Jeanette and Suzanne would often ride Roger double. One afternoon the girls were in the front yard on Roger and the crop duster came swooping over the fields. Roger got spooked and bucked the girls right off his back. He tore around to the back of the house, where the saddle horn got caught in the clothesline, which was attached at one end to the screened-in porch. Roger panicked even more and pulled with all his strength to get loose. Something had to give, and it wasn't going to be Roger. When I got home that evening, the whole backside of the porch was lying on the ground. Thankfully, the girls and Roger were unharmed, but I had a major repair job to do for the Doctor.

. . .

"Get Yourself Back Home"

I was very thankful for work so I could provide for my family. At times, though, the combination of traveling and physical labor was exhausting. During one of these times, Norma Jean and I had an argument. I just seemed to snap. I wanted out of all this! I got angry and said, "I just can't take it. I'm getting out of here." I got in my car and started driving, fully intending to leave it all. I hadn't gotten more than ten miles, though, before I began to question what I was doing. I turned off at the next town, went into a restaurant, and ordered a cup of coffee. Before the coffee was gone, I said to myself, "Glenn Marks, you can be awfully dumb, but you can't possibly be dumb enough to leave your wife and four kids. Get yourself back home, apologize, and get this straightened out." I drove home as fast as I could and found my good wife standing at the door. I blurted out my apology, and we worked things out. We have now been married almost sixty-five years and are so very thankful that in this, as in many other situations, the Lord brought us safely through.

BUILDING CHURCHES

I grew up in a carpenter family: my great-grandfather, grandpa, daddy, and brother all chose that profession. My grandfather had a hammer and nails in my hands when I was very small, maybe only three years old. Yet somehow, farming always seemed more interesting to me than carpentry. I don't know how I could have been so disrespectful to my father and mother, but one night I said to them, "I would rather go fight Hitler than be a carpenter."

Well, I was sent to fight Hitler, and as a medic I was in the thick of the fighting. After the war I went to Bible school, intending to go into the ministry. When I finished school and started in ministry, my intention was to leave all secular work behind and be a real preacher's preacher.

It never seemed to work out that way, though. As we started new churches, there was always some building project or repair that needed to be done. For the first three churches the Church Extension Director was carrying the responsibility for the buildings. When we went to Indianapolis, the first building was contracted, and I didn't have much responsibility. When we got ready to build the church building, one of the men in the congregation was going to take charge of the construction. Then he had a heart attack the week before we were ready to start. He had to give up all extra activity, and we were forced to ask, what do we do now?

The options were to postpone construction or have me take charge. We had a growing congregation with a high of 210 attendees in our house chapel, and we needed more room badly. To stop the building project seemed unthinkable. I was praying about it at my bedside, and an indescribable assurance flooded my soul: If I would trust the Lord and go ahead, I would receive the help I would need to supervise construction and carry on my pastoral duties. I had also recently read Exodus 35:30-35, where God gave Bezalel and Oholiab special wisdom and ability to build the tabernacle. I was able to believe that if God had done it for them, He could do it for me. We went ahead, and the building project went unbelievably well.

When we moved to Lowell, MI, we were taking a break from ministry, and I needed a way to make money to support the family. I had been in contact with a pastor who wanted to build a church. I was able to get plans and help supervise the volunteer labor from the men of the church. The building went well, and the cost was very low, so other churches wanted my help. That's how I got started in the ministry of building churches full-time. I did some traveling, working with a church building company (Church Builders Incorporated out of Grand Rapids) that furnished plans and worked out with the congregation what my fee would be for helping them build. I supervised their volunteer labor and did what was necessary with the other contractors. This became an adequate source of income for my family.

I liked the work, I really did. It just fit. I liked being with people. When a job would open up, the first thing I would ask was to meet with the congregation and talk to them. I would tell them that I couldn't promise anything, but that my experience was that if everyone would pledge themselves to do what they could and trust the Lord, He would add the rest of what was needed. I developed a reputation: "No one builds churches cheaper than Glenn Marks." A man from one of the churches I was working on told the men I was working for, "I don't care what you're paying Glenn Marks—it isn't enough."

The biggest reason for my success at building churches is that I prayed often. If I had a problem, I would write it on my yellow pad on the way home and ask God for wisdom and direction. Almost always, I would have the answer in the morning. One of the churches I was building needed a very large air conditioner unit on the second level near the center of the church. I was told that it would be necessary to get a helicopter to put the unit in place. That would cost about $1,000. I would also need a concrete pump to put in the concrete base for the AC unit, which would cost about $200. The Lord showed me that by leaving a section of the building open, a crane could place the AC unit instead. Also, a well driller in the congregation had the equipment that would lift the ready-mix cement to the second level, so at least $1,000 was saved. Thank you, Jesus!

There were two churches that had a time of questioning about my work. When I heard about it, I immediately asked to meet with the board or the building committee, whoever was in authority. I said to them, "If my negligence or lack of ability has cost money, I want to make it right." We got together with that attitude, and in both instances it wasn't my fault.

Special Building Projects

A lady in our church sold her property (almost ten acres) to a new, large store that was relocating there. She found a nice lot and contracted with a builder for a house. The basement walls were put in, and then work stopped. The builder talked the lady into giving him more money so he could complete the house sooner, but then he declared bankruptcy. The lady

Major Supervision of Building:

1. Wesleyan Methodist, Marshall, MI
2. Lamotte Missionary, Marlette, MI
3. Calvary Baptist, Owosso, MI
4. Chapel Hill, Union, MI
5. First Baptist, Laingsburg, MI
6. Giles Road Baptist Church, Muskegon, MI
7. Bethel AME Church, Saginaw, MI
8. Christian Missionary Alliance, Saginaw, MI
9. True Vine Baptist Church, Saginaw, MI
10. Perry Baptist Church, Perry, MI
11. Baptist Church, Rockford, IL
12. Baptist Church, Three Rivers, MI
13. Good Shepherd, Grand Rapids, MI
14. Port Sanilac Baptist Church
15. First Assembly of God, Wyoming, MI (2 parts)
16. Adrian Black Congregation (Ivory Simms)
17. Wesleyan Church, Muskegon, MI

Built While Pastoring:

1. Edison Park (Redeemer), South Bend, IN
2. North Manchester, North Manchester, IN
3. Providence, Lawrence, IN (Indianapolis)
4. Evergreen, Lowell, MI (3 phases)

Specific Sections Built:

1. Alton Bible, Lowell: steeple
2. Ypsilanti, MI: steeple
3. Hartford, MI: steeple
4. Marquette Missionary Church: laminated beams
5. Memphis Free Methodist: hung doors

Houses I Helped Build:

1. Harry Dawes, North Manchester, IN
2. Sharon Whaley, Lowell, MI
3. McCaul's garage, Lowell, MI
4. Cumberland manor (3 buildings)
5. Glenn (2 South Bend and Ada)
6. Tom Marks, Osceola, IN
7. Gerig, Lowell, MI (2 phases)

Altogether I worked on a total of forty building projects that not only helped others, but also helped us meet our financial needs. I would like to acknowledge that these things could not have been accomplished without special help from the Lord, and also the help and support of my good wife and family.

was stuck without anything.

As a church, we were very concerned and burdened about her needs. She had a handicapped son, and they were living in a motel. One Sunday night when I went home from church, I felt strongly impressed to get out my yellow pad and start writing down the names of people and companies that might help complete the lady's home. I almost filled a whole page. The Holy Spirit encouraged me to go ahead and start the project.

I began contacting people on my list. One of the local TV stations got involved. Two attorneys gave their time, and one of them found money from the builder's assets. Materials were donated. Craftsmen donated their time. The home was completed as good or better than planned, and the lady and her son had many good years in it before they went to heaven.

Another somewhat similar story happened at the same church. One of the families had taken over the husband's father's auto mechanic business, and the building, which had a flat roof, leaked terribly. They had no money, and they had been told it would cost $20,000 or more to fix the problem correctly. The Holy Spirit gave me the courage to "stick my neck out" and begin to fix the roof. With volunteer labor and excellent prices on material, everything was completed for about $8,000. This has been a good testimony to a lot of people.

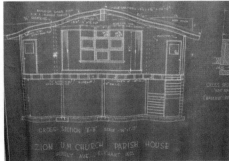

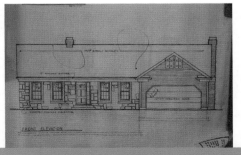

MY PONIES

God's time is the right time. My heart is so full of praise to our wonderful God that I just have to share it with you. If you're reading this, please rejoice with me and praise the Almighty God.

I happen to be one of those people that our Creator gave a strong love for horses. Some of my farming ancestors had this love, and it became evident to me that I also had it. Some of my earliest recollections show this. As a child I wanted a pony, but it was during the Great Depression, and it would have been an additional burden on the family budget. The things you do not get for yourself you want to get for your children, so my pony craze later became an obsession. It became almost unbearable when a neighbor got a pony for his children. I had a good place to keep a pony, and one was actually available for me to purchase. Satan whispered to me, "He got a pony for his kids—what about you?" Then the Holy Spirit checked me just as definitely as could be: I should not get that pony, it would cause trouble in the church and hinder our ministry. I didn't understand it, but I went into my study and prayed, "Lord, you've been so good to me, and you don't owe me anything, but I would really appreciate it if you would either let me get the pony or take away my desire." The desire left me, and my peace returned. I still liked to see ponies, but the need to have them was gone. It was a miracle, it really was!

About three years later, with no thought whatsoever on our part, a pony became available to us. By that time our ministry situation had changed, and it was very evident that it was time to get the pony I had always wanted. We had recently moved into our farmhouse in Lowell, so conditions were better than ever. The problem of not having the money was quickly solved by a neighbor offering to pay for the pony if I did some work for him on his farm to pay him back.

The kids didn't know they were getting a pony.

Top: Sonny, Misty and I at Oak Hill in 1998.
Middle: My granddaughter Hannah and I.
Bottom: Ponies with Hannah, Andrew, and Ben.

Covered wagon ride at Oak Hill 2003, with Pam and Ally Marshall.

Instead of telling them right away, we put the pony out in the barn and told them we were going to have a "special visitor." We took them out to meet the special visitor, and we made a big deal out of it. They were thrilled! It was a very exciting day.

In no time at all, the pony was paid for. Hay and oats were available as a gift from our landlord. With unbelievable ease, in the Lord's time, we had our pony! A couple of months later she had a colt, so then we had two ponies. We eventually sold the colt, but I bred the mare with our neighbor's stallion, and in eleven months we had another pony. And it doesn't stop there! My brother-in-law's uncle had a team of ponies with a wagon, harnesses, and saddles. He hurt his back and didn't want to take care of them

any longer. He was trying to sell them for $600, which was a good price for everything. I didn't have the money, so finally I said, "You know, Buck, I don't have $600, I'm sorry, but I could give you $200." He took it, so now we had four ponies and four children! It was a beautiful team. We had a couple hundred acres of farmland, and the kids rode the ponies quite a bit on the roads and trails out back.

From the beginning I recognized the Lord's hand and blessing, so I promised to use the ponies for his work as much as possible. If a time came when it became a problem to take care of them, I would gladly give the ponies up. Instead of becoming a problem, it only became easier. We were able to buy ten acres of land and build our own house at an unbelievably low cost. Over the years, seven different neighbors let me use their land to pasture our ponies. This was partly possible because one neighbor paid to have a large tube put under the road. Another neighbor sold us hay every year at a very reduced rate.

Remember the neighbor who got a pony, which Satan used to torment me? He only got to enjoy his pony for a few months before it got sick and died. Over the years I have noticed that most families keep their horses for only a few years, until they tire of them or it becomes too expensive to care for them. On the other hand, I have gotten to enjoy four generations of ponies, or a total of fourteen ponies over forty-three years. Fourteen grandchildren have gotten to enjoy them, too!

Because I was so full of joy at how the Lord worked this out, and since the cost of care has been so minimal (about two games of golf a year), keeping my ponies always brought me more pleasure as time went on. However, realizing that a time would come when I could no longer keep my ponies, I began to pray for direction from my Heavenly Father. Branch Adventures in Saranac, MI, came to mind as a possible answer. My letter to them, in which I

considered donating the ponies and equipment to them, was received as an answer to prayer and as a great encouragement. The ponies, harnesses, saddles, cart, and covered wagon will continue to be used in the work of the Lord. I am exceedingly thankful and happy. Praise our wonderful Savior Jesus Christ!

Left: Ponies pulling a sleigh through the snow.
Right: Misty pulling me in our pony cart in 1985.

"Take delight in the LORD, and he will give you the desires of your heart."

Psalm 37:4

Ponies	Cost	Selling Price	Equipment	Cost
Ginger (mare)	$75	$75	Harness, wagon, 2 saddles	$100
Buffy	$0	$50	Other harness	$25
Windy (mare)	$0	$75	Horse saddle	$25
Queenie and Princess	$100	Trade	Cart	$50
Dandy	$0	Died 1 day old	Wheels, lumber for wagon	$75
Cloudy	$0	$0	Miscellaneous tack	$75
Prince	$10	$50	Total:	$350
Sonny	$10	Died 32 years old		
Thunder	$10	$35		
Lightning	$10	$50		
Misty (mare)	$10	Gift		
Star	$10	$150		
Medallion (horse)	Trade	$100		
Cookie	Gift from Church	Gift		
Total:	$235	$585 (Profit $350)		

Sixteen people made substantial contributions to make the care of the ponies easier and less costly, including family members, neighbors, friends, and a veterinarian. The profit I made from the ponies was enough to cover the cost of their purchase and the equipment needed for them, so the ponies ended up costing me nothing.

BUILDING OUR BEAUTIFUL HOME AT OAK HILL

After a few years at Meadowview, we began looking for land to build our own house. While studying a township map, I found forty acres of vacant land. I contacted the owner, an older woman, and expressed our interest in buying ten acres of this beautiful wooded land. There was another interested buyer, but for some reason the owner did not want to sell to him. She gave us a price of $5000. "We really like the property," I said, "But we will have to put in quite a long lane to get to the best building site." She brought the price down to $4,500!

My brother, our son Tom, and I set to work building a 2,800 square foot Cape Cod walkout. With occasional help from friends, we did everything ourselves except finish the drywall and install the countertops. With my brother as guarantor, we borrowed $20,000 to build, but in the end we only needed $19,000. When we asked to have our loan reduced, our elderly banker was very surprised. "I've never had this happen before. I've only had customers come in asking for more money!"

The most enjoyable project of the house was laying the stone front and the stone fireplace. The kids and I collected stones from the property and my grandparents' land. I split the stone, threw it in the trunk of my old Chevy, and brought it home to see if it could be used. Norma Jean helped to decide the placement of the stones and I laid them.

The Lord permitted us to live in our home at Oak Hill for forty-two years. We cherish the memories, especially of Christmas gatherings with the whole family. Our hearts are full of praise to our Heavenly Father!

BUILDING AND BEING BLESSED AT EVERGREEN: THE EARLY YEARS

The miracle of Meadowview encouraged and refreshed our hearts, and it wasn't long before the Lord gave us a renewed sense of purpose. We watched and prayed for opportunities to serve and share Christ. As a family we got involved with a Missionary Church in Grand Rapids. Besides building churches, I made myself available as a supply pastor for area churches.

We were deeply grateful to be in Lowell and wanted to see if there might at least be interest in a Bible study, and eventually even a church in the area. A new housing development was being built close by. As I had done so many times before, I went to the neighborhood to introduce myself and get acquainted with the families.

On the first day, I met a young mother, Bonnie Weststrate. Her husband Herm had recently gotten out of the service and was now working for Bell Telephone. They had one young boy and a baby on the way, and they were just moving into their new home. Neither of them attended church regularly, but starting a family was making them think about the importance of spiritual things. Norma Jean and I became closer acquainted with them, and they indicated that they were interested in a Bible study. We felt we should have two more families, which we soon found, and we started a Sunday night home Bible study. We encouraged these families to join us on Sunday mornings in Grand Rapids.

More families joined the Bible study. In the summer of 1976, I helped one of them build a garage. One of his friends saw it, and I helped him build one that was larger and even a little nicer. A member of the study was impressed and said, "This is so nice,

we should have church in it!"

Others in the group were enthused with the idea, but my first reaction was to panic. I was supervising the construction of four churches at that time. The thought of adding a sermon each week, plus all the other things I knew it would add, seemed like too much. What would I do? Fortunately, I had learned to take it to the Lord in prayer. As I was praying, the Holy Spirit flooded my heart with an assurance that is really indescribable. I knew we should go ahead and start morning worship services and call ourselves a church. I had confidence that the Holy Spirit would help me with my sermons.

We continued having services in the garage until cold weather hit. We did not feel we could heat the garage and make it comfortable, so we moved to the high school. This worked very well for our growing

Several ladies involved in Norma Jean's Bible study

group. It also provided the opportunity for Norma Jean to start a women's community Bible study.

One snowy morning the janitor was not able to make it in to open the school for us. The high school principal and his wife came in to open it up, and they stayed for service. Marlene was their babysitter when their children were young, so we were acquainted with them. Afterwards, the wife was talking with Norma Jean and mentioned that she really wanted to find a women's Bible study. This had also been on Norma Jean's heart, so they agreed to start a community Bible study in the principal's home. Norma Jean continued the Bible study for twenty-five years, and it brought several families into the church.

God was working in the community and in the hearts of people. A lady and her son joined our group and were very active. Her husband, however, was not interested. He was quite a heavy drinker, and drinking was a big part of his life. His wife had almost given up on him.

Summer was coming, and we were beginning to think about camp meeting. At ladies' Bible study, Norma Jean quite casually said, "Why don't you invite your husband to go to camp meeting with us?" The woman reacted with complete shock and assured Norma Jean that he would never do that. We all began to pray for him.

To everyone's great surprise, the man went to camp meeting with his wife and son. Together they attended the evening evangelistic services. Hearing the Gospel message brought true conviction to this man's heart, but no altar call was given. Quite a heavy storm came up that night, and the man was very frightened that the big trees near the cabin would blow down on them. It made him even more aware of his mortality. He spent a miserable day and went to the service again in the evening, having made up his mind that he would not leave the tabernacle until he got things right with the Lord. When the altar call was given, he immediately went forward, confessed his sins, believed Jesus, and became a new man. That was the complete end to his drinking, and he started working for the Lord.

Interestingly, his main reason for going to camp meeting was because beer was cheaper in Indiana than in Michigan, so he had planned to fill up his car with cheaper beer. Also, he had gone to camp meeting as a teenager, but his interest had mainly been the girls. Even so, the Lord used this good camp meeting experience from his younger years to prepare his heart. We have such a great and patient God!

Good things were happening at the church, and we finally had enough of a congregation that we knew it was time to start building. The church owned ten acres of land next to Oak Hill, but some big problems surfaced with that property. The right-of-way was not correct, and we couldn't get a building permit until the road was improved. No matter what I tried, I hit a dead end. This frustration, together with exhaustion from traveling and building churches, brought on a state of discouragement and depression.

A new District Superintendent was elected, and he came to see us. I unloaded my frustration on him. We had gone to college together, he had started a church, and he had been a foreign missionary, so he understood. In a few days, he came back to me with a request: "Let's look at Luke 13:6-10, Jesus' parable of a man who had looked for fruit on his fig tree for three years. Because he found none, he wanted his gardener to cut it down, but the gardener replied, 'Let's give it another year.'" The superintendent asked us to give the church another year, and we agreed.

Then another good thing happened. We went to camp meeting again. My good wife was so concerned about me and my depression that she worked it out for the evangelist and I to spend some time together. We sat in chairs under one of the big beech trees and talked. The preacher tried several times to get the conversation on positive things, but I had a negative, depressed answer for everything. He had been to our cabin and met the family. Finally, almost in desperation, he said, "Reverend, you have four teenage children, don't you?" I brightened up a bit when he began to talk about the kids. He went on to say, "Reverend, if you have four teenage children who are all serving the Lord, you must have done something right." That statement was enough for me to hang onto. I was able to resist the devil, and he had to leave me alone. I got my fire back, and I was able to listen to the Holy Spirit's ideas about how we might be able to build a church.

Not long after that, we got tentative approval from the township authorities to build. That night, the man across the street, who had always wanted the property the church had, came to me and said, "Reverend, that isn't the best place to build a church. Why don't you look for another property?" He was a lifelong resident, so I looked at him and said, "You know the area. You find us a piece of property, and we'll see what we can do."

In about a week he came back with an offer of eight acres to trade for our ten acres. It turned out to be the land I had unsuccessfully tried to buy earlier. I always thought it was the best possible place to build. The trade was made, and both of us were delighted. The first thing I did was put up a sign saying, "A New Missionary Church Will Be Built On This Site For The Glory of God."

So now we had the property, but what were we going to do with it?

Putting up our sign at groundbreaking for Evergreen Missionary Church, November 2, 1980.

THE OLD-FASHIONED BUILDING BEE

Our family had moved to Oak Hill, and we had a group of believers and a property on which to build a church, but we needed to decide what to do. Then the Lord gave me an idea. My grandfather and great-grandfather were both old-fashioned barn builders. They hewed out the timbers, and then the men from the neighborhood would come together and have a building bee to erect the building in a single day. I had a desire for years to do this on a church building, but it had never worked out. Finally, the time seemed right. I believe that the Holy Spirit assured me that this was the time to do it.

The Lord gave me courage, so I stuck my neck out, drew up some plans, and talked to Joe Kimble at a conference. I showed him what I wanted to do, and he told me they had just built a similar building. So he gave me those plans. Now I needed to present the plans to my congregation and see if they thought I was still sane or if I had gone off the deep end. I had preached a sermon a few weeks before based on 2 Chronicles 20:12. A great host of enemies had banded together and were ready to attack Israel. King Jehoshaphat prayed, "We do not know what to do, but our eyes are upon You." This prayer had become a motto for us. When I presented the idea of "a church in a day" to my people, they were willing to follow my leadership.

Now I was ready to present my idea to the district executive board. A group of us from Lowell went to a board meeting. I asked the board to guarantee us a loan for $40,000. I also asked for permission to contact the district churches and ask that each man consider giving a day's wages or a day's labor to help build our church. The district superintendent said, "Thank you, Glenn. We'll check it out and get back with you." So we started putting on our coats to go home, but then one of the men from our group said,

Groundbreaking at Evergreen Church with Frank Miller, Herm Westrate, and Warren Smith.

"Sit down and wait a minute—there's a motion going on back there!" From the time I presented my idea to the time they approved it was less than half an hour!

I was given permission to present my idea at the district conference. They were meeting at our church campground over in Brown City, and when I pulled up and parked, a man came running up to me. "Glenn, Glenn, Glenn, I hear you want to build a church!" I said yes. He said, "I've got some money to help build churches, and I'd like to loan you that money!" It was about $3,500. I was able to take that as confirmation that God was in it and that He wanted me to do this, so I was able to present my plan at conference with confidence.

We got the permission we needed, and we were planning to construct a 40'x90' building. We laid the block for the foundation, put in the underground heating and plumbing, and got ready to pour the concrete floor. Three brothers who were concrete finishers volunteered their time. There was

Would you be willing to join an

OLD FASHIONED BUILDING BEE

to help build

The Missionary Church at Lowell, MI.?

Would you Give. . .

✔ a day's wages?

✔ a day's labor?

"For we are laborers together with God" I Cor. 3:9

- -

I'll be glad to:

☐ Give _____ day's wages   amount _____

☐ Give _____ day's labor   trade _____

☐ Other _____   **Mail to:**

Name _____   **Glenn H. Marks**

Address _____   **10268 Foreman Rd.**

_____ Phone _____   **Ada, MI 49301**

Make checks payable to Michigan District Missionary Church, Lowell Account

equipment at the local gravel pit to mix concrete, so we figured out how to put that to use. We hauled water from the river. On a Saturday, with volunteer labor, we mixed, poured, and finished the floor, the covered entryway, and the curbs at the street. A local concrete company set the curb form at no charge. In one day we saved more than $2,400.

We set the date, Saturday, August 8, 1981, for the old-fashioned building bee to erect the building. People said to me, "Are you going to set a rain date?" I said, "No, because if this is of the Lord, He'll take care of the weather." When the day came, it rained on the east side of us, it rained on the west of us—four sides of us, but we just had a little shower to cool it down a bit. The Lord took care of it.

Recently, I had become tired of traveling and being away from home, so I found a job with a local contracting firm. Just before the building bee, my boss called me in and said, "Glenn, I have to do something that I have never done before. I have never had to lay off any of my carpenters because of lack of work, but I must lay you off for a while." That was wonderful news for me. I could draw unemployment and have full time to work on the church.

We didn't get electricity until two days before we were ready to have the building bee. We had everything in, but the electric company hadn't hooked it up. So on Thursday and Friday we cut some material, and on Friday night at six o'clock we started nailing together walls and partitions. My dear brother Don had far more experience than I did, so I said to him, "Don, take charge of this project and figure out what needs to be done, and I'll get crews to do it." He accepted. Don prefabbed the whole gable end on Friday night. Assembling it on the ground made it much easier to do—we would just have to lift it up the next day. It had the siding on and the whole works. Now we were all ready to go.

The Lord laid it on the hearts of forty-six people to come on Saturday. At dawn we picked up the gable end and began placing the trusses on the building. A crew worked on each side of the building placing siding to give stability. Another crew began putting the plywood sheets on the roof, and still another crew began laying roof shingles. A different crew put in windows and doors, and yet another crew built the roof for the front entrance. It seemed that the people who came were just the right balance of crew leaders and helpers. We found jobs for everyone. My brother even gave a hammer to the newspaper reporter! The ladies served wonderful meals, and some of the ladies worked on the building. One of my important jobs during the day was to go to all the crews and keep them rejoicing. "The joy of the Lord is our strength."

At dark on Saturday night our church building was completed. It was rough on the inside, but we were able to hold a Sunday evening service in that building. People who drove past the church on Saturday morning were amazed to see the completed building when they went past in the evening. We were featured on the evening news on the local TV station. On Monday there was a newspaper picture in the local lumber company with the caption "A Church in a Day." A local builder saw this and said, "A church in a day? No way." But it had happened!

Jesus Christ was glorified with this miraculous project. Enough money was donated by men giving a day's wages to pay for the labor that needed to be hired. The cost was about $40,000, or $11 per square foot. Praise our wonderful Jesus!

Grand Valley Ledger · Wednesday, Aug. 12, 1981 · Page 4   **Churc**

Helping hands erect church

The new Missionary Church, 10501 Settlewood Drive, became a reality in just one weekend. Volunteers began construction of the building last Friday night at 7 p.m. Forty men and their families were able to complete enough of the building that services were held in it for the first time Sunday evening. Pastor Glenn Marks was pleased by the progress and enthusiasm for the old-fashioned Building Bee. The church was officially organized in November, 1980, meeting in the high school until now.

ARTHUR J. TAYLOR: A LETTER

Fern and I have lived in the Grand Rapids area for almost forty-five years, and we have known Glenn and Norma Jean almost from the time we arrived. Glenn and I go back about sixty-five years, to when we both attended the Fort Wayne Bible Institute. We were both there in 1947 and 1948. This wonderful college is no longer operating, but it was not our fault that it closed. It then became Taylor University of Fort Wayne.

Glenn and I have worked on a lot of churches together down through the years. I left the full-time ministry after twenty-five years of building and planting churches. I worked over twenty-five years, full-time, in God's work, just building churches throughout the nation—in Florida, Virginia, Pennsylvania, and many in Michigan. I recall Glenn and I working on a church in the Flint area, and we were up on a scaffold, about forty or more feet up in the air. Glenn reached out to grab a bar, but there was none there, and it was at that time God got hold of Glenn as he was about to fall to solid cement below. We still don't know just how Glenn kept from falling except that it had to be the mercy of God on his life. We were putting a spire up on a church in Indiana when a big storm was heading our way, and the lightning was flashing. Somehow, we were able to get it anchored before the storm hit. We had about three to five minutes to do it, and it was done. The church that was built under Glenn's ministry in Lowell was done in a couple of days. Glenn had all of the underground work done, and we had a work bee. Glenn appointed me and his brother, and the three of us headed up different crews. Most of the church was built in one day. This was because of Glenn's supervision.

Glenn and his wonderful family were in the church I pastored in the Grand Rapids area. They helped in a wonderful way for well over a year. Glenn filled the pulpit several times while I was away. I know that one can't always paddle the canoe by himself and that we each had a wonderful helpmeet. Norma Jean was always there by Glenn's side. We can't give enough credit to our terrific wives.

I could go on and on, but those are some of the great times we had down through the years.

Rev. Arthur J. Taylor

BUILDING AND BEING BLESSED AT EVERGREEN: THE LATER YEARS

Our new church, which we built through an old-fashioned building bee, was originally called Lowell Missionary Church. We later changed the name to Evergreen. There was great enthusiasm up to this point, and fortunately it did not diminish when we needed to finish the interior of the building. Somehow, this phrase got started regarding volunteer labor: "The pay isn't so good, but you can't beat the retirement plan." It was said very lightly, but it did have an influence.

Three events were especially encouraging as we finished up both the inside and outside work around the new building. The first was concerning the last $10,000 we needed to borrow. It had been promised to us as soon as a man got an insurance settlement. That seemed real good, but the settlement was delayed. We had a fairly large bill at the lumber company, and the manager had been exceedingly patient. All of our other bills had been paid on time, but we could not pay this one. Finally, the manager said, "Before this runs for three months, I will need to put a lien on your building." I answered him with a confidence only the Lord can give: "Go ahead and do what you have to do, but I still believe we will make this payment before that is necessary." In a very short time the District Superintendent was speaking at a church, and a lady said to him, "I am so glad you are here. I have some money I want to loan." She wrote out a check for $10,000!

I had been laid off right before the building bee, but this gave me the opportunity to work alongside the others as we finished things up. I brought my tractor and equipment over to do a lot of the work on the grounds, so very little needed to be hired out. I remember so well the day I said to the man working with me, "I believe when we are finished today, I am going to take my tractor home." The second encouraging event came less than an hour after I got home. My boss called and asked me to come back to work on Monday. That in itself was a miracle of God's timing, but the reason he wanted me to come back was to clean out quite a large building that had been a store and make it into offices. The lights, suspended ceiling, and some other things were in very good condition, and they were things we needed for the church. I asked if I could load them up in my truck instead of the dumpster. That was no problem, and these materials saved the church at least a couple thousand dollars.

Lastly, as the building project was drawing to a close, we were ready to drywall. A men's group at another church had collected $1,800 and given it to our building project. I contacted the owner of the drywall company I had used before, and he did not have any work at the time. When I offered him the $1,800 for hanging and finishing the drywall, he took it and was very thankful for a nice winter job. Things were soon completely finished, and we dedicated the building in July of 1982.

We continued our ministry at Evergreen for twenty-seven years. The Lord blessed the work, and many families and individuals came to know Christ on a new or deeper level. We tried to keep the children's and adult ministries both meaningful and relevant. For several years, a group of men and I went to the county jail on Sunday evenings and ministered to the inmates.

Bible quizzing became an important part of the youth ministry. Two of the families in leadership had children the right age and became involved in

the quizzing competition. They brought home many first-place trophies in both state and international quizzing. Later, nine of our fourteen grandchildren were involved in Bible quizzing and, again, many first-place trophies were awarded to their teams.

The time came when we needed more space, especially classrooms. We were debt-free at the time and could have borrowed money, but we wanted to avoid a loan if possible. "Building without borrowing" was our prayer, and with God's help that was accomplished.

Throughout all of my ministry, both at Evergreen and our other churches, I did not see myself as especially gifted in any one particular area. I saw my role in ministry mostly as a helper. God was my Helper and I was just the Lord's servant, here to help!

By 2003, we had been able to help the church begin its final building project of a larger sanctuary. We knew, however, that it was time to bring our work at Evergreen to a close and retire from full-time ministry. Building and ministering at Evergreen was a blessing for which we are deeply grateful, and we pray that the Lord will continue to bless others through it.

MICHIGAN MIRACLES

The Lord brought us to Michigan in a miraculous way, and we have seen other miracles here. These are just a few.

It was a miracle that we were able to rent the farmhouse at Meadowview Farm.

It was a miracle that we could buy land and build our house at such minimal cost.

It was a miracle that the very first family we called on while praying about a church plant in Lowell was looking for a church family. They have remained faithful to the Lord and the church for over forty years.

It was a miracle that our youngest daughter Cindy and her husband Stan were led to move to the area and help with the church. They were extremely hesitant, wanting to be sure that it wasn't personal preference or family ties that brought them.

It was a miracle when one of the women of the church went in for surgery and was informed that she didn't need it. Physicians at the University of Michigan had told her she needed surgery on her neck. The church felt a heavy burden of prayer for her healing. When she went in for surgery, the doctors could not explain it, but she did not need the surgery.

It was a miracle that we could build our church building in one day. The only way it could have happened was that enough people, with enough skill and energy, were brought together with enough will and purpose to make it happen.

It was a miracle that we could build phase II of the church without borrowing. We were out of debt and could have borrowed money, but we believed the Lord that He would help us build debt-free.

It was a miracle that the Holy Spirit prompted me to call on a neighbor family one evening. The children were acquainted with our grandkids and had come to church a few times with their mother. It was later in the evening than I usually made calls, but I felt strongly that I should go to the home. When I entered, the father was sitting at the table looking at a telephone book. I talked a little with the wife and kids, but very soon the husband and I also started talking. We seemed to have a lot of things in common, and I invited him to come to church with his wife and kids. He came the very next Sunday. Our relationship grew, both the man and his wife recommitted themselves to Jesus, and they became a big help in the church for the next three years. I never knew until much later that the man was looking at the telephone book to find a room to stay in because he had decided to leave his wife and children. I was so thankful I had obeyed the Holy Spirit and made that call.

LOWELL REFLECTION

As we look back on our years in Lowell, our hearts well up with thankfulness. Our homes at Meadowview and Oak Hill were truly a gift from God. Meadowview is now a horse farm, and the huge barns are full of horses. Oak Hill has been sold to a young family. The father is a builder and teaches construction at a local college.

Evergreen Church continues to minister in the community of Lowell. Pastor Rick Ferguson, who came after me, pastored for nine years and, among many other things, completed the third and final phase of the church building.

While we were in the process of moving from Lowell, a new pastor, Dr. Bill Hossler, came to Evergreen. He had recently retired as the President of the denomination and wanted to move to the area to be close to his children and grandchildren. He had previously been a District Superintendent, and before that a pastor of a large church in Michigan, and before that a young, new pastor at a church plant in Ohio. He was the one who took the church in Ohio when we moved to Pontiac!

We serve a great God. Praise God from whom all blessings flow!

"Take delight in the LORD, and he will give you the desires of your heart."

Psalm 37:4

"And my God will meet all your needs according to the riches of his glory in Christ Jesus."

Philippians 4:19

PRAIRIE CAMP

Camp Meeting has always been a priority in the Missionary Church and in my life. Prairie Camp, near Elkhart, Indiana, is the North Central District camp. I have attended Prairie Camp every year of my life except one: when I was a combat medic in Germany during World War II. My first trip was in 1925, when I was only three weeks old. My mother tucked me in a market basket, and my family traveled from Union, Michigan, to Prairie Camp in my grandfather's new Model-T Ford!

Prairie Camp is a family camp with activities and services designed to minister to all ages, from infants to seniors. The first meetings were held in tents. There were large meeting tents and family tents that attendees called home for ten days. Families came from all directions in horse and buggies or farm wagons, many bringing along the family cow to provide milk for the children.

A permanent tabernacle was built in 1927, and it was a masterpiece of construction for that era. The large steel beams made possible the spacious building with few posts to obstruct the view. As a child I enjoyed playing in the sawdust on the floor. In the late 1940s I worked with my brother, cousin, and two uncles to pour and finish the concrete floor. The tabernacle has since been enlarged.

Biblical teaching and preaching has always been the central focus of camp meeting. Many, young and old, have "hit the sawdust trail" to the altar to make decisions for Jesus. Many pastors and missionaries can trace their ministry to a call at camp meeting.

Here's how a typical day at Prairie Camp has gone in recent years: The day starts bright and early at 7:00 AM with a prayer meeting. After breakfast there are classes and services for everyone. Babies are cared for in the nursery, while children all have classes and activities. Teens have their own morning service in the big youth tent. Adults can get a free cup of coffee and attend lecture series and Bible studies.

Afternoon holds a variety of activities, including rallies, crafts, games, a carnival for children, and field trips and service projects for the teens. In the evening the tabernacle fills up—with many sitting outside—for the evangelistic service. Teens join the adults, sitting front and center. Children have their own meetings, and the nursery is in operation. Many people respond to the altar calls for salvation, consecration, and other spiritual or physical needs.

The afterglow service is another tradition at Prairie Camp. When the evening service is over, people gather around a huge bonfire and enjoy free refreshments (ice cream, popcorn, chili, etc.) and music by various groups. It is a great time to visit with friends, and it makes for a pleasant ending to a wonderful day.

In the past I have served eight years as night watchman and then later as Camp Pastor, which gave me the privilege of presiding over prayer meetings, both morning and evening, and overseeing the altar services. In addition, I was "Grandpa Glenn" and told Bible stories to four different groups of young children: three-year-olds, four-year-olds, five-year-olds, and kindergarteners.

Every year, Prairie Camp is a time of learning, growing, and spiritual refreshment. If you have had the privilege of attending a camp meeting before, thank the Lord for such a wonderful tradition and blessing. If you have never attended a camp meeting before, I highly recommend it!

Clockwise from top left: Norma Jean and I with our grandchildren at camp in 1996. Prairie Camp cabins in the 1950s. Me ziplining in 2008. Inside the tabernacle. The Marks family at Camp Meeting in 1996. Inside our cabin at Prairie Camp.

FORREST AND JEAN SHUCK: A LETTER

People influence our lives in many ways. Those influences shape the person we are and the person we become.

Such is the case with my friendship with Glenn and Norma Jean. We mutually shared the love of our Lord and Savior Jesus Christ through our ministry. Having the fellowship and friendship of another ordained minister is so valuable.

My first memory of Glenn and Norma Jean was their work in starting a church in North Manchester, Indiana. They were very dedicated to the church, seeing the church grow, but most importantly, bringing people to know the love of Jesus Christ. They have always given unselfishly to the Lord's work.

Our friendship dates back many years. One of the most memorable of those times is the fellowship we shared at the Indiana Campground every year during the ten-day annual camp meeting. Our cottages were right across from each other. While our children played together, Glenn, Norma Jean, my wife and I had many wonderful times together talking about the Lord's blessings and the challenges we all faced. The campground days are some of the most wonderful memories I have of our friendship.

While our paths haven't crossed for many years, our friendship always remains. The memories always bring a smile to my face.

May God continue to bless Glenn and Norma Jean. We will always appreciate your friendship and the fellowship.

Your friends in Christ,

Forrest and Jean Shuck

November 9, 2013

THE BRIDGE BUILDER

An old man going a lone highway,
Came, at the evening cold and gray,
To a chasm vast and deep and wide.
Through which was flowing a sullen tide
The old man crossed in the twilight dim,
The sullen stream had no fear for him;
But he turned when safe on the other side
And built a bridge to span the tide.

"Old man," said a fellow pilgrim near,
"You are wasting your strength with building here;
Your journey will end with the ending day,
You never again will pass this way;
You've crossed the chasm, deep and wide,
Why build this bridge at evening tide?"

The builder lifted his old gray head;
"Good friend, in the path I have come," he said,
"There followed after me to-day
A youth whose feet must pass this way.
This chasm that has been as naught to me
To that fair-haired youth may a pitfall be;
He, too, must cross in the twilight dim;
Good friend, I am building this bridge for him!"

Will Allen Dromgoole

MY CARS

While serving in the military, I saved money and planned to buy a new car immediately after returning. As much as I wanted that new car, when I returned home I didn't really need one and instead felt the Lord asking me to give money to a friend who was going into missions work.

When I eventually needed a car, I was able to write out a check for $1,450 and buy a brand-new, light green, four-door Plymouth Deluxe! It was a beauty, and it served us well.

We had several cars over the years. Many were used, but some were new. We gave up one new car, but the Lord permitted us to have twelve new cars. I have always seen this as just one example of God keeping His promises to His children. Luke 6:38 says, "Give, and it will be given to you. A good measure, pressed down, shaken together and running over, will be poured into your lap." Praise God for His good gifts!

SAYINGS THAT HAVE AFFECTED MY LIFE

- "If I can control myself, I can control an army." —Napoleon Bonaparte

- "Even the turtle won't get anywhere unless he is willing to stick his neck out."

- "Where there is a will, there is a way."

- "Necessity is the mother of invention."

- "If someone else can do it, I can too, even though it may take me longer."

OUR CHILDREN

Norma Jean and I were really given a hard blow when we lost our first baby. Everything seemed to be going well throughout the pregnancy. However, when Norma Jean went into labor, the doctor gave some wrong advice and continued with his neglect and lack of attention. About four days later our beautiful, fully-developed little girl was stillborn.

Norma Jean was devastated, and Satan really jumped on me. "Is this the kind of God you serve? You gave up a lot, $100 a day, to take this church for $25 a week. Why don't you go back to your business?"

We soon learned that not everything is good, but that "all things work together for good," as stated in Romans 8:28. Norma Jean spent a month with her grandmother, who was a real saint and had gone through worse things than this. Grandma had a lot of experience helping to mend broken hearts. One of her sayings was, "Now, now dear, this too shall pass." Norma Jean got a lot of help, and before long we were expecting another child. I got involved with building another church and our home. I was able to resist Satan and his suggestion that I quit. I am sure that our ministry was enlarged through all of this.

Our daughter Jeanette was born just as we were getting involved at North Manchester. When she was a month old, on a cold, snowy evening, we took her along to a prayer meeting. She made a big hit that night and was always a big help in our ministry. She became a cardiac nurse. While attending Columbia Bible College she met her husband, David Oliphant,

Marks family, 1961.

a dedicated and gifted man from Tennessee. He is a pastor and Environmental Engineer. Together they have pastored a small church, and Jeanette has worked with Good News Clubs and helped start a church in the Hispanic community. They have two sons.

Our second daughter, Marlene, was born while we were in North Manchester. She was a timid girl but still greatly loved by the people of the church. When we moved to Indianapolis and her big sister Jeanette started school, Marlene wanted to learn what her sister had learned. Jeanette liked to teach, too, and before Marlene went to school, she could read whatever Jeanette was reading. It must have been good for both of them, because they were both valedictorian of their classes.

Marlene graduated from college with a teaching degree in Elementary Education. While teaching in Michigan City, IN, she met her husband, Lars Sjoholm, an intelligent, fun-loving Thermodynamics Engineer from Sweden. They are both musical and enjoy being involved with music in their church and community. They have three children.

Tom, our only son, was also born while we were at North Manchester. We were really happy for a boy, and he was a very good boy. He especially enjoyed playing with his fire trucks. He worked incredibly hard helping with Oak Hill. One time I gave him a pile of used lumber and asked him to build a garden shed patterned after our barn. He pulled the nails from the lumber and built the shed.

While attending Bethel College he worked in the maintenance department, and after college he was hired there full-time. He became Head of Buildings at the college. While at Bethel he met, for the second time, a lovely, good-natured young woman named Becky Allen. Their first meeting, they discovered, had been at the hospital nursery when they were born! They married and have three children. They have been very active in their church, especially in Bible quizzing and children's ministry.

Our fourth child is Cindy, and she was born while we were in Indianapolis. She was not exactly expected at the time, but our wonderful Heavenly Father knew that she was the one we needed, and we have always been exceedingly thankful for her. Tom and Cindy were very close in age and were constant playmates as children. Cindy loved all of our animals and was involved in their care and training much more than the other children.

Cindy became a Labor and Delivery nurse and married a kind, creative young man, Stan Gerig. He grew up in Jamaica, where his parents were missionaries. Stan is a respiratory therapist. They have six children, and the whole family has been a great help in music, the children's work, and leadership at Evergreen Church.

Norma Jean and I have thanked God again and again for each one of our children, their godly spouses, and the grandchildren.

"But from everlasting to everlasting the Lord's love is with those who fear him, and his righteousness with their children's children."

Psalm 103:17

SUGGESTIONS FROM GRANDPA MARKS

Christmas 2001

1. Make sure you have been born again. Mom and Dad's religion will not get you by.

2. Read and obey the Bible (Joshua 1:8).

3. Always be totally yielded to Jesus. Remember, living sacrifices tend to crawl off the altar.

4. Always put the work of the Lord first (Matthew 6:33).

5. Learn to be content and thankful for what you have (1 Timothy 6:6). The prosperity of the Lord consists not in the abundance of the things we possess, but in the fewness of our wants.

6. It is probably God's will for you to have a life companion. Never get in a hurry or question God if you haven't found yours yet. Keep busy serving the Lord, doing his will and work. My observation is that this is the best way to find a mate. Remember, you can have a happy and fulfilling life if being single is God's choice for you.

7. Never date or marry an unbeliever. Never marry a new Christian. Give them plenty of time to prove themselves.

8. When it comes time to marry, make sure that both of you are committed for life. Commitment will last; other things may lose their luster.

9. Guard that the things that attracted you to each other don't become a source of irritation.

10. Don't be a dropout for any reason.

11. Make Christ the head of your life and home at all times.

MY GRANDPA

Robbie Sjoholm, age 10

1999

To pick the one person that I respect and admire the most was definitely the hardest part of this assignment, with so many people in my life that encourage me to live the right way, but the one person that always pops into my mind is my grandpa, Glenn Marks. He never really tells me to keep trying or to work hard, he encourages me by what he does and the example he sets.

My grandpa lives with my grandma in a large house that always makes you feel at home, tucked deep in some of the misty woods in Grand Rapids, Michigan. At age 76 he still pastors a small church nearby. He is a great carpenter but always uses that gift for other people having built many churches, his own house, and many other houses and small buildings. He also uses his hands to make many of the gifts he gives. One Christmas when I was little he gave me a little, wooden rocking horse that I will always cherish because it reminds me of him and it came from the heart (not to mention its quality was better than any from the store).

My grandpa always wants to make people happy and if someone asks him to do something he does it even if he is half asleep. He's one of those people that if you make him smile you forget all of your worries and fears, but if you make him sad you feel as guilty as a criminal. One of the things I'll always remember about him is his persistence to finish everything he starts no matter what. He has a great sense of humor, the wisest person I know, and he always does the right thing. My grandpa may be considered short at 5' 4", but his heart is way too big for that.

MOTHER PIG

Before Norma Jean and I were married, I wanted to make a cutting board for her to use. My mother had gotten one in the shape of a pig, and I used that as a pattern to make each of my siblings one as a gift when they got married. I wanted to use the same pattern for our board. I found a very nice red oak board with a lot of grain, and I used that. We have used it for the past sixty-four years, and it has served us well.

I used our pig board as a pattern for making one for each of our children as a wedding gift, and they have all enjoyed having it. One day, I got the idea to make a pig board for each of our grandchildren. I remembered I had some lumber my brother gave me from a tree that grew on my Great-grandfather Diethrich's farm. I discovered it was a white oak, which is what the colonial ship "Old Ironsides" was made of. A very hard wood like that would be ideal for cutting boards for the grandkids, and it would be of special significance that the tree had grown on their great-great-great-grandfather's farm.

With the use of our son Tom's equipment and some help from him, we made them in two or three days. We have been giving them to our grandkids on their wedding day or when they set up housekeeping. I am so thankful that the Good Lord let me do this.

THE FUTURE

Many years ago I heard the saying, "We don't know what the future holds, but we know who holds the future." A few years ago I noticed Psalm 31:15: "My times are in your hands..." I do not remember how or when these thoughts were brought to me, but I have lived with them long enough to know the absolute truth of both.

In the natural world, there are many things that would cause concern and worry. Just to name a few, the environment seems to be changing. The national debt is very scary. The political situation seems so unstable. The idea of political correctness has many people afraid to confess Christ and to witness for Him. We have physical conditions that have the potential to be extremely challenging.

But the Bible tells us that "God is faithful; he will not let you be tempted beyond what you can bear" (1 Corinthians 10:13). It also says, "Surely your goodness and love will follow me all the days of my life, and I will dwell in the house of the Lord forever" (Psalm 23:6). This promise is our guaranteed future.

"My times are in your hands..."
Psalm 31:15

"God is faithful; he will not let you be tempted beyond what you can bear."
1 Corinthians 10:13

"Surely your goodness and love will follow me all the days of my life, and I will dwell in the house of the Lord forever."
Psalm 23:6

LESSONS LEARNED AND SHARED

> *"Blessed are those who hunger and thirst for righteousness, for they will be filled."*
>
> Matthew 5:6

These are the big lessons I've learned in my life, and the ones I want to share with my grandchildren's generation and the generations that come after.

Seek first the Kingdom of God and His righteousness. Our desire and motives should be like Mary's when she said to the angel, "I am the Lord's servant. May it be to me as you have said" (Luke 1:38). We must come to the end of ourselves to the point that we're the Lord's servant regardless of what that means. For her it could have meant giving up her home, her marriage, and her very life. She probably didn't understand all that was happening, and we won't understood all that happens in life, but by faith we have to believe and really commit.

Romans 12:1 says, "In view of God's mercy, offer your lives as living sacrifices." One of the problems with living sacrifices is they tend to crawl off the altar. I tried to get away, but life brought me to the place where I had to realize I was absolutely helpless. The best way to break a horse is to put him in a situation where you tire him out. You can't teach a horse anything until he's tired. The disciples in the ship were completely worn out and hopeless after the storm (Matthew 8:23-27). Jesus came in with a great miracle, and then they were ready to listen and learn. If we really want to follow Jesus, we must make a full commitment and not give up under tribulation and the testing of our patience. Difficulty works patience and a lot of other things in our life.

None of us are adequate for the task, but the Holy Spirit gives us the strength for the task. John 3:34 says that God gives the Holy Spirit without limit. Without Christ we can do nothing, but with the Holy Spirit on us He can empower us. That's what He did with building the church in Indianapolis. Also, when I started the church in Lowell, I was supervising four churches, but the Holy Spirit gave me the assurance He would help me with my messages. And I believed Him. We have to believe the promises of God—really believe them, not just recite them. God's Word is not just printer's ink on paper, but it's the living, powerful Word of God. We must believe it and move forward where He leads.

WE DO NOT HAVE A CHURCH, BUT WE DO HAVE A MINISTRY

> *"They will still bear fruit in old age."*
>
> Psalm 92:14

When my wife and I retired in 2003 after fifty-three years of ministry, which included starting five Missionary Churches, I had only one regret: that I didn't believe the Lord for even greater things. We stayed in Lowell for ten more years, and during that time we just naturally wondered what was ahead. Fortunately, we had seen the promise in Psalm 92:14: "They will still bear fruit in old age." God helped us to cling to that promise, and we have been willing to believe the Lord for his leading.

Norma Jean continued to teach Sunday School until December 2010, when she retired after teaching for sixty-five years. She still has some contact with those she had in the thirty years of weekly Ladies' Community Bible Study. She is a good grandmother to our fourteen grandchildren, too.

Having been a combat medic in World War II, the VFW (Veterans of Foreign Wars) became of interest to me in my retirement. I was not interested in the organization over the years because I had the idea that it was just a place for veterans to get together, drink, smoke, and share their troubles, like in a local bar. Much to my pleasant surprise, in Lowell there was a group of men who, along with the men from the American Legion, wanted their new building to be smoke-free and to have no bar. I had the privilege of being chaplain of both organizations, and at the monthly meeting of the VFW I had the privilege of leading in prayer. The adjutant's (secretary's) thirty-two-year-old daughter was murdered, and I was able to help him greatly. The quartermaster (treasurer) knew the Lord as a teen but had accumulated a lot of spiritual baggage, which I helped him shed. The commander was a man I led to the Lord, and who helped us start the church in Lowell.

As a veteran, I have been privileged to speak at high school assemblies. More than once I have been blessed to speak to six classes of seventh grade history at the local school in Lowell. I was also invited to share my war experiences with about 4,000 people at an Amway convention in Colorado Springs. On the same trip, I ministered to about forty people one-on-one or in small groups. I have appreciated the privilege of telling of God's protection while I was with the first troops that entered Germany.

Every couple of months I spoke at the nursing home and the retirement home in rotation with other ministries. And there were still many, many times when I was blessed to talk with someone about spiritual things, either to challenge or to encourage. I continued to attend Prairie Camp each year, and I have been privileged to be Grandpa Glenn to the pre-school children. In 2009, I took my ponies to camp and arranged for every child who wanted a ride to get one.

Norma Jean and I have been able to take Psalm 23:6 as our promise for the future. Goodness and mercy will follow us every day of our lives, and then we will dwell in the house of the Lord forever.

Written July 2013

LESSONS FROM SCRIPTURE

In 2007 or early 2008, shortly after Norma Jean turned eighty, we read Psalm 90:10 about "forescore years." We decided we should admit we were old. Then we read Psalm 92:14, which states, "They shall still bring forth fruit in old age." We took this as a promise and a goal for the remainder of our lives. The Lord seemed to confirm this to us by giving us Psalm 23:6: "Surely goodness and mercy shall follow me all the days of my life: and I will dwell in the house of the Lord for ever." We took this promise to mean that nothing could come to us unless it was covered by His "goodness and mercy."

When Norma Jean started to show signs of dementia, we were very surprised. I had never thought of that possibility, though her mother had that problem and had spent considerable time in a nursing home. Another Scripture came to mind as the dementia progressed. Romans 8:28 says, "And we know that all things work together for good to them that love God, to them who are the called according to his purpose." Early in our ministry when we lost our first baby, we learned that things do not have to be "good" in order to "work together for good."

This verse met our need for quite some time, but as the condition worsened we needed more help, and I discovered another verse. Acts 5:41 tells us that the apostles were "rejoicing that they were counted worthy to suffer shame for his name." I realized that my suffering was very minor compared to what many of God's children were going through, but the thought helped.

As Norma Jean's dementia continued to worsen, I needed more help. 1 Peter 1:7 came into focus: "That the trial of your faith, being much more precious than gold that perisheth..." Throughout most of my life, $35 an ounce was the value of gold. Now the value is around $1,170 an ounce, so suffering has really increased in value!

The next verse the Holy Spirit brought to my attention was Colossians 1:11: "Strengthened with all might, according to his glorious power, unto all patience and longsuffering with joyfulness..." This is a tremendous promise. With His might and power, we can handle things with "patience and long-suffering," not just enduring it but with "joyfulness." This has helped a lot.

My most recent challenge from God's Word has been the account of Jesus coming to the disciples in the ship, which is recorded in all four gospels. Matthew's record is in 14:22-33. Jesus told the disciples to "to get into a ship, and to go before him unto the other side." The Scripture tells us that the wind was so strong that it kept them in the middle of the sea. I am sure that the exhausted disciples thought that something had gone terribly wrong. In reality, the only thing that had happened was that the contrary winds had kept them in the place where Jesus miracle could be greatest and do the most good.

Jesus had not been with the disciples, but he had controlled every wave so it could rock the ship and show the disciples their great need of help. However, the waves were not strong enough to sink the ship. When they first saw Jesus coming to them walking on the water, they said, "It is a spirit." Of course, Jesus could not help them when they had this false view of him. He said, "Be of good cheer; it is I; be not afraid." After Peter walked on the water and "they were come into the ship, the wind ceased." Everyone in the ship "worshipped him, saying, 'Of a truth you are the Son of God.'"

We have no idea what the future holds, but we are confident that no matter how strong the waves and how hard they rock the ship, we as a family will make it safe to the other side. That's because "greater is he that is in you, than he that is in the world" (1 John 4:4). Also, I believe that because of these circumstances all of us will know Jesus better and be able to depend on Him more.

A CORD OF THREE STRANDS

"A cord of three strands is not quickly broken."

Ecclesiastes 4:12

A Letter to Norma Jean on our 64th Anniversary

My Norma Jean,

It has been quite a long time since I have written anything to you, so I wanted to write for our sixty-fourth wedding anniversary this 8th of June, 2014.

The memory of freshman orientation early in the 1946 school year at Fort Wayne Bible Institute is still as fresh in my mind as ever. Our wonderful Heavenly Father had it all worked out so that the empty chair was beside you, and He put an override on my timid nature and desire to be alone. He caused me to go sit beside you. The Lord had also prepared your heart, or you very easily could have been much more surprised and cautious than you were.

I really believe that the only reason our courtship made it was because we both had this intense desire to serve our Lord Jesus Christ. Jesus had planned that He wanted us to join together in the marriage bond because that would be the most complete way we could serve Him.

To make this relationship come to completion, the Almighty had to apply the principle of Ecclesiastes 4:12: "A cord of three strands is not quickly broken." When your strand and my strand became very, very weak, the powerful strand of Jesus held us together until our strands could become strong again.

When the root of a tree is broken by the force of the wind, the tree will grow back two roots, and it becomes much stronger. Our love is like that. It has been made strong enough to take us through our entire life.

All My Love,
Glenn

AFRICAN HUT/AFRICAN CHURCH

Sorting through some things in the attic at Oak Hill brought back a very vivid memory when I came across a hand-built African hut. I was in a "throw things out mood," but behind that African hut was too much of a meaningful event for it to be trashed.

When I was in grade school, for an assignment in social studies, each class member was to represent something about the lifestyle of the African people we were studying. I remember seeing some pictures of the African huts on high supports to keep them out of the water. My heart became set on making a replica of that for my project. My attempts to build or draw the African hut did not go well. I was praying that God would help me get the project done. It came down to the night before the due date, and still no African hut!

Dad returned home from a long commute, where he had worked physically hard on the construction of a new church building. As a younger child, I really believed that Dad could build or fix anything. I do remember thinking at this point, though, that it was too late to ask Dad to help me now. I was desperate. Dad really did like to help us kids with anything he could. When I finished explaining to him the project and my desire to have the African hut on supports, he immediately went to work.

The next morning, Dad willingly took the extra time to drive me to school so I would not need to take my finished project on the bus. I was so thankful to God and to my Dad. I was smiling from ear to ear, proud to be able to present my Dad-built African hut! My teacher knew what happened and still gave me an A for the project!

This event happened over forty years ago. Countless other events have happened where I ended up taking up Dad's offer to "C.O.D." (Call on Dad!). I have deeply appreciated Dad's help over the years. Not only have I benefited from his help, but other family members, church family, and several others have benefited as well.

Dad and Mom are now living in an assisted living facility. Even though he is technically retired, he is still eager to help others. God has guided him to raise funds to build churches in Mozambique, an African nation. I imagine those dear people will be thanking God and smiling from ear to ear when their African church is completed!

By Cindy Gerig

November 2013

My dad-built African hut, minus the thatched roof.

GERALD STEELE: SELECTIONS FROM A LETTER

Pastor Glenn Marks led me to Jesus. The year was 1962, and I was fifteen years old. I was attending camp at the North Central District of the Missionary Church's campground, located approximately seven miles south of Elkhart, IN. While I had grown up in a godly home, I was not serving Jesus. Like most teenagers, I had gone to camp to have a good time. At that juncture in my life my primary interests were sports and girls. The camp provided an opportunity for both. However, on the first Wednesday night of August, God got my undivided attention.

After the evening service I returned to the boys' dormitory with a friend whose name was Lester Rassi. His sister had popped a big sack of popcorn for him, and he was sharing it with me. We actually were in our beds, munching and talking. The talk elevated to conversation of a more spiritual nature. It was after 10:00 pm, and the boys' dormitory was still abuzz with conversation. It must have been after 10:30 pm, and Pastor Glenn, who was one of the appointed night watchmen, stuck his head through the door and told us to cut the noise and that he was going to cut the lights. Boldly, Les spoke up and said, "Pastor Marks, Gerald and I are having a serious discussion about the Lord." At that juncture he responded, "Boys, why don't you get dressed and go with me to the tabernacle." Quickly, we did. Once we were in the tabernacle we made our way to the front row, and there brother Glenn openly shared the gospel with me. Finally, he looked at me and said, "I think this boy wants to pray." He was spot on, and within a matter of a few short minutes I was openly weeping and confessing my sins to God. Within a short period of time I knew that my sins were forgiven and that I was a new creation. I remember looking at the clock, and it was exactly 11:15 pm. I knew at that moment that I was born again.

One year later at that same camp, I was filled with the Holy Spirit and God called me to missions. I have had the joy of ministering on four different continents: North America, South America, Europe, and Africa. I am presently the lead pastor at Pleasant View Missionary Church, Greenville, OH. This marvelous congregation of approximately four hundred is also helping me with a ministry in East Africa, in the country of Mozambique. In 2006 I started working with a group of pastors in the northern part of that country, teaching them on how to launch disciple and church planting movements among the Makua people. Today, as a result of these efforts, nearly 52,000 disciples have been made, and 633 churches have been planted.

Glenn's and my paths have crossed on numerous occasions throughout the years. Just recently he approached me regarding the passion that he possesses to help plant churches in Mozambique. At eighty-eight he told me, "I still have a desire to bear fruit in my old age." Glenn's entire ministry career has been devoted to church planting, so it just seemed logical to him that he could help plant "granddaughter" churches in Africa. So, he in his late eighties and me in my late sixties are partnering in this venture. It's truly amazing! We have come full circle. I'm sure brother Glenn would say, "To God be the glory."

December 30, 2013

CHURCHES IN MOZAMBIQUE

Norma Jean and I never went on any foreign mission trips. We always wanted to, but either didn't have the money or the time. We have always had a heart for overseas missions, though, and we encouraged support and involvement in our churches.

I still had a desire, though, to help. How could I fulfill it?

Well, about fifty years ago I led a man named Gerald Steele to the Lord at Prairie Camp. He and his wife Miriam worked as foreign missionaries for years, first in Brazil and other places, but most recently in the African nation of Mozambique. They launched their ministry in that country in 2006, and seven years later there were over 50,000 disciples and approximately seven hundred new churches established. Their strategy is the hub model. Instead of a pastor just starting a church like we did, the challenge for a new pastor is to find five or six other men, teach them, and expect that they're going to start their own churches. That's the way this whole thing has worked.

One time at camp meeting I saw Gerald walking across the campground toward me, and he had another man with him. He said, "Glenn, Glenn, I've got someone I want you to meet. I want you to meet your grandson!" I was confused, because this man had a different skin color. "Well," Gerald said, "You led me to the Lord, and I led him to the Lord, so he's your spiritual grandson!"

When we moved into Hubbard Hill, I said to myself, "What in the world am I going to do?" Then I remembered that I'd heard about this from Gerald. I said, "I wonder if I could raise some money to help over there. Maybe that would satisfy my desire." I contacted Gerald, and he sent me a letter about how thrilled he was that I wanted to do it. So Evergreen took on the project of raising $5,000 to build a church over in Africa. By the help of God, that money and another $15,000 has been raised. I'm tremendously thankful to the Lord that He allowed me to be involved.

New church building in Mozambique.

RUTHIE MILLER: A LETTER

Glenn Marks is our uncle and my mother's brother. Here are just a few of the things that we appreciate about him and Aunt Norma Jean.

One thing is the sayings Uncle Glenn repeats from Grandpa. Our nephew is small for his age. I am not sure he even makes the growth charts. Becky reminds us that Uncle Glenn said that our Grandpa told him, "You can never tell by the size of a frog how far he will jump!"

When I think of the little children growing up in today's world, I often think of the verse Cousin Tom said Uncle Glenn pointed out to him: "Thy faithfulness is to all generations."

Uncle Glenn recalls many happy childhood memories and is such an enthusiastic storyteller. I enjoy hearing the stories and his detailed explanations of how things used to be and how things used to work.

When I was little, my mother never wanted my brother to overdo on teasing us. She said her brother Glenn teased her so much—why, one day he even locked her in the corncrib. My mother said it was because she would cry, and she finally caught on that if she did not react, she would not be so fun to tease. Still, she did not want that to happen to her children. So Uncle Glenn's teasing probably spared me from (some) teasing.

But that is not why I am writing this. What impressed me is when some years later I heard him tell my mother how sorry he was for teasing her. "I don't know why I teased you so much, Sis—locking you in the corncrib and all..." I wonder if more siblings could be humble enough to apologize for the way they treated the other, could they be more free to remember the good times? I thought it very commendable of Uncle Glenn to do that.

We all appreciate how concerned and caring Uncle Glenn and Aunt Norma Jean were to us during the time of our father's and our sister's illnesses. They and their families sent flowers and generous gifts of money and helped in other ways.

We are happy that Uncle Glenn and Aunt Norma Jean have moved close by and look forward to more times together.

Ruthie Miller for the family

RELFECTION UPON REACHING OLD AGE

After reaching eighty, we had to admit we had come to old age. But we had the promise that we could still bear fruit in our old age. That has been a tremendous promise. Since we came to Hubbard Hill, Mary's and the angel's statements have meant so much to me. I've had the privilege of bringing forth fruit here by talking to people at the dinner table, starting a service in health care, starting prayer groups for couples and singles, building churches in Mozambique, and writing this book.

Simeon also encourages me in old age. He was righteous and devout. Our righteousness comes from Christ, and being devout means really digging into our faith. He was waiting for the consolation of Israel, so he had the right desires and ideas. The Holy Spirit was upon him, so he had the right relationship. He was at the right place at the right time, with the right things to say, and other people cooperated to help him honor Jesus. Mary and Joseph brought him to the temple at the right time. That's been a challenge to me. I don't know what the future holds, but I will bear fruit in my old age. The only ending I know to old age is dying and going to heaven.

"They will still bear fruit in old age, they will stay fresh and green…"

Psalm 92:14

"'For no word from God will ever fail.'

'I am the Lord's servant,' Mary answered. 'May your word to me be fulfilled.' Then the angel left her."

Luke 1:37-38

"Now there was a man in Jerusalem called Simeon, who was righteous and devout. He was waiting for the consolation of Israel, and the Holy Spirit was on him."

Luke 2:25

I want to give special thanks to each of my family members for their prayers, support, help, and encouragement in writing this book. Two of our daughters spent countless hours making this book much more interesting and readable. Thank you, Marlene and Cindy, for using your God-given abilities in such a remarkable way!

This book is protected by copyright laws. However, permission is granted by the author to copy pages for use in ministry.

All proceeds above the cost of printing, shipping, and tax will be used for building churches in Mozambique or other ministries that build God's Kingdom.

For further information about these ministries or other questions, write to:

glennmarksbook@gmail.com

or

Evergreen Church
10501 Settlewood Dr.
Lowell, MI. 49331
Attn. Glenn Marks Book

Glenn Marks
Hubbard Hill
574-296 4128

"Now to him who is able to do immeasurably more than all we ask or imagine, according to his power that is at work within us, to him be glory in the church and in Christ Jesus throughout all generations, for ever and ever! Amen."

Ephesians 3:20

Made in the USA
Charleston, SC
19 December 2014